Air Fare

AIR FARE
The Entertainers Entertain

Allan Gould

Wine tips by Tony Aspler
Illustrations by Graham Bardell

CBC Enterprises/Les Entreprises Radio-Canada
Montréal · Toronto · New York · London

Published by CBC Enterprises/Les Entreprises
Radio-Canada, a division of the Canadian Broadcasting
Corporation, P.O. Box 500, Station A, Toronto (Ontario),
Canada M5W 1E6.

Publié par CBC Enterprises/Les Entreprises Radio-Canada,
une division de la Société Radio-Canada, C.P. 500,
Succursale «A», Toronto (Ontario), Canada M5W 1E6.

To the best of our knowledge, the recipes in this publication
are original, unless otherwise indicated.

Canadian Cataloguing in Publication Data
Gould, Allan, 1944-
Air Fare : the entertainers entertain

Includes index.
ISBN 0-88794-157-5

1. Canadian Broadcasting Corporation—Biography.
2. Radio broadcasters—Canada—Biography.
3. Television personalities—Canada—Biography.
4. Cookery.   I. CBC Enterprises.   II. Title.

PN1990.7.G68 1984   791.45′092′2   C84-099518-0

Publisher/Éditeur: Glenn Edward Witmer
Editor/Révision: Betty Corson
Managing Editor/Direction de la rédaction: Robert Daley
Designer/Conception graphique: John Murtagh
Food Consultant/Conseillère en alimentation:
Dorothy Ferguson
Illustrator/Illustration: Graham Bardell
Typesetter/Composition: Trigraph
Printer/Impression: The Bryant Press Limited

Printed and bound in Canada

1 2 3 4 5 / 88 87 86 85 84

*Cover photos: Roy Bonisteel and Luba Goy
in Elite Confections*

CONTENTS

Introduction and Wine Notes

*W*hen you switch on your favourite CBC television or radio program, you invite a familiar face or voice into your home. The men and women who host the shows become part of the family. Now, through *Air Fare*, they repay the favour by inviting you into their homes, into their lives, and specifically into their kitchens.

To compile this collection we approached well-known CBC personalities across the country. As publisher, I would like to thank those who agreed to open their doors for us and give us a glimpse of their lives away from the studio lights and microphones.

There is one thing that the media stars share with the rest of us: they tend to get hungry around mealtime. From these candid portraits of CBC celebrities, it's obvious that they enjoy their food and many of them are accomplished chefs. Their favourite recipes, collected in this book, are very personal and revealing, evoking memories of childhood and of experiences past, and current lifestyles.

Read about the stars, try their recipes, and continue to tune into CBC every day for Canada's best air fare. You'll be in good company.

Glenn Edward Witmer,
Publisher

---

*W*hen the publisher, Glenn Witmer, invited me to suggest wines to accompany the favourite recipes of CBC personalities in *Air Fare*, I accepted with alacrity and a waiver from my dietitian. Armed with a corkscrew and an autograph book, I set about the task. After all, how often does a wine writer get to play sommelier to the stars? Mercifully, I was not faced with having to supply wines to accompany anything like Stuffed Beaver Paws, Albatross à l'orange or Whale Blubber Tartar. If faced with the exotic or any extinct species, I gravitate toward an all-porpoise rosé. (No more puns, I promise.)

Most of the personalities who opened their hearts and pantries to Allan Gould confess to liking a glass of wine with their meals. Some are connoisseurs; others don't really mind as long as it comes from the grape; and one or two prefer Nature's own wine—water (nonvintage, preferably Nouveau).

Given the legislation governing the consumption of alcoholic beverages in Canada, you will not see anyone in a TV commercial actually consuming wine or beer. (Have you noticed that Wayne and the boys never get to drink the beer at the summer cottage or that the Spumante Bambino girl does violence to her partner but never to the product?) To watch television, you'd think that wine is a table decoration that stands next to the flowers and is poured merely to make more washing-up for the hostess.

For radio, matters are less complicated. When I had a wine spot on the local CBC Toronto afternoon show, *4 to 6*, I would bring along a different wine every week for the host, Jim Wright (whose profile and recipes appear on pp. 152–55). In true radio fashion, where sound is all, I would make great play of pulling the cork and pouring the wine as close to the microphone as possible. Jim and I would taste the product and discuss it. (Judging from his recipes, Jim has a very sweet tooth and for nine months I was bringing him nothing but dry wines!) Despite all the noises we made, the program used to get letters asking if we really did taste wine on the air or were we just using sound effects.

In selecting wines or the appropriate beverage for the recipes contained in this book, I kept one thought in mind: choosing a wine is like choosing a marriage partner—the choice has to complement and set off the mate. Even those who couldn't tell Beaujolais from Bull's Blood have heard of the old adage "white wine with fish, red with meat," or the more subtle variant "white meat, white wine; red meat, red wine." Like all clichés, there is a grain of truth in both sayings—but they are too rigid and all-embracing. If you live by these maxims you won't come to any harm, but you'll miss out on a lot of wine-drinking pleasure because they preclude so many delightful combinations (a sweet Sauternes with paté de foie gras or Roquefort cheese, for example, or port and Stilton).

There is a good reason for drinking white wines with fish: the oils in certain varieties can make red wine taste metallic. The crisp acidity in dry white wines enhances the flavour of shellfish where the fruitiness of reds would work against it. But salmon poached in red Burgundy and served with the same wine is delicious. Which all goes to prove there are no rules except one: what your palate likes in terms of food and wine is ultimately right.

Choosing from the hundreds of wines made around the world, you can find any number that can be served with each course, from soup to nuts. If you plan to offer more than one wine at a meal, keep in mind that the sequence should be as follows: white before red (except for sweet dessert wines); young before old; dry before sweet. If you want to serve a single wine throughout the meal, the best choice is a dry Chardonnay (white Burgundy) or dry Riesling. Or if you can afford it, Champagne,

Certain foods and seasonings are the enemies of wine because their strong flavours will impair the taste in combination. Grapefruit, pickles, lemon juice, vinegar, and strong sauces like Tabasco, curry powder, and excessive garlic are antipathetic to wine. Eggs, bananas, and chocolate don't do much for wine either.

In some cases where wine is inappropriate, I have offered suitable alternatives. In one or two instances I have indicated that it might be beneficial for the chef to consume a sufficient quantity of beverage alcohol before the fact—to work up enough courage to tackle the recipe in the first place. If wine (the most natural and healthy of beverages) is proscribed for medical, religious, or philosophical reasons, you can always take it in pill form—as grapes.

Tony Aspler

Air Fare

Pierre Berton

The man who loves a Challenge credits his wife for their fabulous meals

*I*f any group of Canadians were asked, "Who is the most famous citizen of our country?" I suppose that a far larger number would say Pierre Berton before they would mention any prime minister, rock star, or hockey player. And if the overused term "Renaissance Man" has ever been used properly, it has been when it is affixed to that broadcaster, historian, social critic, lecturer, newspaperman, and author.

Although Berton has written over two dozen books, including his famous *The National Dream* and *The Last Spike* (the latter, a winner of the Governor General's Award for nonfiction in 1971), his voice and face are probably best known from his regular appearances on *Front Page Challenge* on CBC-TV, which he joined in the fall of 1957. ("They had auditioned everyone except me," he recalls. He received $125 a week for doing the show, back at the start.)

Born in Whitehorse, Yukon, on July 12, 1920, the ubiquitous author-cum-TV-star fell into broadcasting with the same ease that he has shown in his dozen other fields. "It was in Vancouver, in 1946; the city was having its sixtieth jubilee. Jack Scott asked me to do four radio broadcasts—fifteen-minute talks on the city." He was "broke; just out of the army," and newly wed to Janet Walker, with whom he would eventually have eight children and two grandchildren, as of the fall of 1984.

Berton had studied radio speech at the University of British Columbia, from which he was graduated in 1941, and his first job was as a reporter on the *Vancouver News Herald* that same year. He threw himself with ease into radio work: he did *City Desk* once a week, telling stories on CBC Vancouver, then wrote a thirty-minute radio play (*Byline Story*; "Mavor Moore produced it; I had a small role"). Then it was off to Toronto, in June 1947, and a partial list of his work there could have provided two dozen trivia questions for his recent board game, Tour de Force.

"I needed the money, so I did a lot of TV"

He talked about the Klondike on CBC radio ("which led to writing books about it"), guest-appeared on a number of shows, was a panelist on *Court of Opinion* ("with Lister Sinclair—we were classmates at UBC") for the fabulous sum of $35 a week, worked for CBC's International Service, wrote a series of radio plays and several documentaries—the list goes on forever.

It was truly inevitable when television came to Canada that Pierre Berton would be there, smiling into your living rooms. But, brutally frank as always, he declares that "I needed the money, so I did a lot of TV." And for those big bucks—edging up to $100 a week—who could blame him? So he appeared on *This Week, Fighting Words, Tabloid*, and, eventually, *Close-Up*, where he became a regular interviewer of such personalities as Robert Service (of "The Cremation of Sam McGee"

The kids come over for dinner every Sunday, which means "rarely fewer than sixteen," since that always tends to include wives, boy or girl friends, and so on. Berton also takes the children (well, hardly *children*, ranging in age from mid-thirties to low twenties) out for Chinese dinner on birthdays and other special occasions at such places as the Poto, near his office in downtown Toronto ("Northern Chinese, and *very* good!").

He holds strong opinions about almost every aspect of imbibing or partaking. "I drink a lot of Pimm's No. 1—you mix it with ginger ale and 7-Up, a slice of cuke or apple." Or Moscow Mule (ginger beer, vodka, and fresh lime), which, Berton fastidiously notes, "should be served in a copper cup." And the broadcaster/author goes on to crack, "Me and the boys drink a lot of beer!"

Even coffee arouses passionate feelings: "I won't have instant coffee in my house. And I'm insulted if someone serves it! I have a drip machine at home. I like *good* coffee and *good* wine." Regarding the latter, the Bertons serve wine at dinner ranging from reds to Inniskillin Canadian, and "nothing less than good Chablis."

Pierre Berton's profound feelings about food could be held (happily) responsible for his nearly 40 years of marriage: "I would like to say that I married my wife because she liked her roast beef rare. I couldn't *abide* a woman who liked her meat well done! My wife's a *very* good cook, and I like to eat well. We *always* ate well, even when we had no money."

As might be expected, Pierre Berton is a snacker: he makes and devours salted almonds and candied orange peels every Christmas and "I'm a *nut* for Rogers' Chocolates; they're very, very good, and I bring a few pounds back every time I'm out in Vancouver." But running track and lifting weights helps keep the weight down.

One of Berton's favourite food stories is about the eating habits of one of his great heroes, William Van Horne, who was responsible for the building of the railroad back in the nineteenth century: "Van Horne used to wire ahead for two chicken dinners and eat both himself! He was a gourmet and a gourmand."

In terms of the massive creative output of Pierre Berton, as well as his love and appreciation of food, the description is applicable to Van Horne's biographer as well.

fame) and Peter Ustinov. Then came his first appearance on *Front Page Challenge*, and the rest, as they say, is history.

Despite his busy schedule, the Bertons are famous for entertaining—giant Christmas/New Year's parties and "a big party every summer for friends"—about 200 of them—at a barbecue at their home in Kleinberg, just north of Toronto.

KLONDIKE BAKED BEANS

This dish is suitable for sleighride parties, outdoor barbecues, or Sunday brunches. It can also be served, in smaller quantities, as a side dish with sausages, frankfurters, baked ham, or almost any substantial meat.

INGREDIENTS

2 lbs. navy beans	1 Kg
1 lb. lean, unsliced bacon	500 g
½ lb. thinly sliced bacon	250 g
2 bay leaves	2
1 bunch parsley	1
6 stalks celery	6
2 cloves garlic	2
1 tbsp. oregano	15 mL
1 tbsp. chili powder	15 mL
6 cloves	6
3 tsp. salt	15 mL
6 large tomatoes	6
1 5½-oz. can tomato paste	1 156-mL can
6 large onions	6
2 cups molasses	500 mL
1 cup sherry	250 mL

INSTRUCTIONS

Soak navy beans overnight in cold water. The following morning simmer them very lightly together with bay leaves (crushed), parsley, chopped celery, crushed garlic, oregano, chili powder, cloves, and salt. Cook until soft (about 1½ hours). To test them, remove a bean or two and blow on it; if the skin breaks, they're ready. Drain off liquid and reserve it. Place beans in a crockery pot or earthenware casserole and add the bacon (or salt pork). Don't use sliced bacon; buy it in a slab and dice it into cubes. Take a few cups of liquid in which beans have simmered, and put this in another pot to simmer. Chop tomatoes and add to liquid. Then add tomato paste. Chop 3 of the onions very fine, and the other 3 into chunks, and add them. When the mixture is hot, pour in the molasses. Pour the result over the beans in the casserole. Put a lid on it and bake for at least 6 hours in a 250°F (130°C) oven. (The longer beans bake, the better they taste.) Check after 3 hours to make sure there's enough liquid. One hour before serving, remove the lid and add the sherry. Take the thinly sliced bacon and cover entire top of the beans. Put the lid on and return the pot to oven. Fifteen minutes before serving, remove the lid, turn on the broiler and crisp the bacon into a covering crust. These beans are best served as a main dish with nothing else except freshly baked sourdough bread, well-buttered.
Serves 10–12

WINE

It may be far from the Klondike but Mexican red wine, or reds from southern Italy, would stand up to this lumberjack of a meal.

Recipe originally published in Pierre & Janet Berton's Canadian Food Guide, rev. ed., © 1974 *Pierre Berton Enterprises Ltd.*

Arthur Black with his dog, Angus.

Arthur Black

The versatile host of Basic Black *confesses that one thing he can't do is cook*

*I*n the clear northern air of Thunder Bay, Ontario, satellites are quite visible. And so, it seems, is Arthur Black. Even the career—to use the term very, very loosely—of Black bespeaks the kind of man who would end up doing the kind of show he is now doing.

Born in Toronto on August 30, 1943, he attended four different high schools, and "semi-left home at sixteen." (Grade 9 was his "last real grade," although that eclectic mind possesses "some elements of 11, 12, and 13—but no parchment.")

Then Black studied radio and TV arts and journalism at Ryerson, where "they taught us to talk so we could sell cigarettes." (It worked, in a way; he smoked for twenty-five years until February 15, 1984, when he had an appendix operation, woke up, "realized that I couldn't breathe," and dropped the habit.) It was not until the age of thirty-three that he entered the world of radio and TV. In between, his various jobs included working as deck cadet on a boat, selling clothes in department stores, selling encyclopedias (for one night), serving as an extra in a Spanish movie, working on a farm, slugging it out in the stockyards of Toronto, even prodding cattle, if not himself. But along the way, there were somewhat related jobs. He was the assistant editor of the *Imperial Oil Review*, for instance, until he asked for a raise and they fired him. "They didn't realize before then that I was even working there."

Then came the epiphany—the moment when a man and his proper (so far?) role in life come together. Almost halfway through the biblical threescore and ten, Arthur Black went to CBC, where "a fellow took a shine to me." The man asked if Black knew agriculture and "I lied and said yes."

So for the countless hundreds of thousands who enjoy *Basic Black* on Saturday mornings, and *Radio Noon* in Thunder Bay, and the Arthur Black newspaper column in seven papers across Northern Ontario, or who have read his witty collection of radio commentaries (also entitled *Basic Black*), we can be thankful for his little white lie. He was given the chance to read the hog market reports, then environmental pieces ("I somehow got quickly labelled 'a noted conservationist'"), and then *Radio Noon* in Toronto.

Then came the job offer to do *Radio Noon* in Thunder Bay; he moved there, hated it, moved back to Toronto, and hated *that* city. Black bravely tried free-lancing it ("I made $79.95 for the entire year"), at which point he decided to give Thunder Bay another chance.

Black married in 1976, his daughter was born in 1977. He was separated in 1979, and now resides with Lynne McClain, a producer of *Radio Noon* in Thunder Bay, of which he is currently host. (Announcer/operator is the classy term for this decidedly unclassy personality.)

Basic Black was and is his first national radio show, it should be noted. And Arthur Black does *not* do TV, and never has. "I have this bald head," he explains. "I was told, 'You'd be good—get a toupee,' but I decided not to."

The national show has been on CBC radio since July of 1983, with steadily rising ratings and interest. And, matching the personality and career history of Arthur Black, it is *not* done in a traditional fashion. After all, the show is done out of Toronto and Thunder Bay via line link, with the

"I made $79.95 for the entire year "

staff in the former and Black in the latter—over 1,000 miles apart. Not that there are not compensations: "You don't have to go to all the production meetings, being out in Thunder Bay," says Black.

Hosting the show is "what I do for money," he admits. "It's not the focus of my life." After all, there is his daughter, his lady, the mountain bike he just purchased. ("It's got gears, and I can go up hills!") And there is his impressive history as a fisherman. "I *think* I'm a fisherman. I hang around the lures at Canadian Tire. I threw my last fishing rod into the rapids. I tried to wade in after, and I couldn't find it. It would have been classier if I hadn't gone after it."

But if you want class, you don't tune in to Arthur Black. It's when you want wit, irony, charm, and a healthy bit of sheepdog lunacy. But, when entertaining, he tends "to fall asleep a lot," which makes him a somewhat less-than-perfect host. "In another life, I may have been a hermit," he confesses.

And another thing: Arthur Black never cooks; the Lasagna and Green Tomato Mincemeat recipes are compliments of his mother and Lynne.

"In another life, I may have been a hermit"

He *does* drink—"everything, especially Scotch and dry red wine." And he eats most things, too—although he'll never forget the day some "Chinese guy" came on his show and cooked something spicy in a wok. "I burned my tongue from the heat, and had trouble getting through the show. I never had him on again."

One of his pleasures is eating at a Finnish restaurant called the Hoito in Thunder Bay ("the breakfasts are huge"), and he enjoys such fine Hungarian places as the Tarogato when he is in Toronto. Cross-country skiing in the winter and swimming every day in the remodelled Y keep him fairly in shape. And, because "I eat anything around," he tends to keep snacks out of the house. "Otherwise, I'd empty the bowl."

LASAGNA

INGREDIENTS

³/₄ lb. pork or beef, cut in large chunks	375 g
¹/₂ lb. sweet Italian sausage	250 g
1 tbsp. shortening	15 mL
1 small onion, chopped	1
1 clove garlic, chopped	1
1 tbsp. basil	15 mL
1 tsp. oregano	5 mL
2 cups water	500 mL
2 5¹/₂-oz. cans tomato paste	2 156-mL cans
¹/₂ lb. lasagna noodles	250 g
1 lb. ricotta or cottage cheese	500 g
1 lb. mozzarella cheese, sliced	500 g
¹/₄ lb. Parmesan cheese, grated	125 g

INSTRUCTIONS

Melt shortening in large heavy pot. Add meat and sausage and cook slowly until well browned. Add onion and garlic and cook until golden. Add basil, oregano, and 2 cups (500 mL) water (or more if the meat isn't covered). Allow to come to a boil and then add tomato paste. Stir. Lower flame, cover, and simmer for 2¹/₂ hours. Stir occasionally and add water if needed. During the last 15 minutes of cooking time, prepare the lasagna noodles according to package directions. Preheat the oven to 350°F (180°C). When the sauce is done, remove the meat from the sauce and place meat in the top of a double boiler. Cover and refrigerate. In a deep rectangular baking pan or casserole, place a few spoonful of sauce. Over this, place one layer of lasagna. Cover with drabs of ricotta, slices of mozzarella, Parmesan cheese, and ¹/₄ of the sauce. Start again with a layer of lasagna, adding the other ingredients in the same order. Make 3 or 4 layers in the same fashion. The last layer should consist only of lasagna, Parmesan cheese, and sauce. Bake, uncovered, for 15 minutes. Remove from the oven and let cool. Cover and refrigerate. Before serving, heat the lasagna casserole at 350°F (180°C) for 25–30 minutes or until very hot. Let it stand 5–10 minutes before cutting and serving. While the lasagna is baking, take the meat in the top of the double boiler from the refrigerator and heat over boiling water for 35–45 minutes. Serve meat separately. If you make a mistake and put the meat in the lasagna casserole along with the sauce, it still tastes great!
Serves 6

WINE

A bottle of Bardolino to transport you from Thunder Bay to the lush Veneto region of Italy. Or Chianti from the Tuscan hills.

GREEN TOMATO MINCEMEAT

INGREDIENTS

4 qts. (5 lbs.) green tomatoes	4 L (2.5 Kg)
2 lbs. brown sugar	1 Kg
1 lb. raisins	500 g
1 lb. currants	500 g
¹/₂ lb. mixed peel	250 g
¹/₂ cup vinegar	125 mL
¹/₂ cup butter	125 mL
1 tsp. cinnamon	5 mL
1 tsp. cloves	5 mL
1 tsp. mace	5 mL
1 tsp. nutmeg	5 mL
1 tsp. salt	5 mL
Wax	

INSTRUCTIONS

Chop tomatoes and drain. Note that tomatoes should be chopped rather than sliced; otherwise the mincemeat goes a little stringy. Cover with cold water. Bring to a boil and simmer for 30 minutes. Drain. Add brown sugar, raisins, currants, mixed peel, vinegar, and butter. Stir well and boil until thick (at least 2 hours or more). Cool mixture and add spices. Keep in glass jars and seal with wax.

WINE

An off-beat wine for an off-beat dish: Muscat of Setubal from the Lisbon area of Portugal, a sweet fortified wine. If unavailable, substitute with a cream sherry.

Roy Bonisteel

This Man is Alive to the joys of cooking

*T*here are certain things of which we can be pretty sure in this world: that the sun will rise tomorrow, that Winnipeg will be cold in February, that TV hosts must live exciting and glamorous lives.

Another theory disproven. Take Roy Bonisteel, for instance—so handsome, so debonair, the host of *Man Alive*, the profoundly thoughtful religious program of CBC-TV since October of 1967. Who would guess that he is the son of a farmer, the youngest in a family of seven sons and three daughters, and that he lives today on a farm, just a few short miles from where he was born and grew up, in Trenton, Ontario, about a ninety-minute drive east of Metro Toronto?

If you guessed, you're pretty good at this sort of thing. And Roy Bonisteel is *very* good at *his* sort of thing, to over one and a half million admirers across Canada every week—and at a new time in the 1984 season: 9:30 P.M. on Wednesdays, following *Market Place*—"a great slot," he says, with uncharacteristic enthusiasm in his deep, authoritative voice.

His roots go deep, both literally and historically: the Bonisteels were "old United Empire Loyalists who came over in 1780, given Crown Land in the Bay of Quinte area." Roy was born on May 29, 1930, dropped out of high school in Grade 11 ("I have five honorary doctorates, however!"), and began to work for newspapers: the Belleville *Intelligencer* and the Trenton *Courier Advocate* (now *The Trentonian*). Just two years later, in 1951, he moved into radio at CJBQ, Belleville, as a DJ and news reader. Then it was off to St. Catharines, Ontario (CKTB), where he did news and interviews on radio for twelve years, from 1953 to 1965. That's *twelve years*, in a field where almost *no one* stays anywhere for longer than three or four. (Check the other stories in this book; aside from Pierre Berton, Betty Kennedy, and Wayne and Shuster, how many have been with *one* show for more than a few years?)

During this time Bonisteel married and had three children. (One is a psychiatric nurse; the second is the editor of the Prescott *Journal*; the third works with the retarded. And all three children, all in their twenties, have generously provided him with three granddaughters and one grandson within the past two years.)

In 1965 Bonisteel began to produce commercials and did a show for the United Church of Canada on radio. "I was the host of interviews and music, current affairs and humanitarian interests. It was nondenominational." It was called *Checkpoint*, and it would prove to be an important background when *Man Alive* came alive.

That same year, while producing that show, he was asked to produce it out in British Columbia and also look after other religious programs on B.C. TV and radio. He was there for two years, until the Centennial Year, when he was invited to come back to Toronto and head up nation-wide radio operations for the Roman Catholics, the Anglicans, and the United Church. "I said that I'd only work for them on a nondenominational basis," says Bonisteel. His condition was accepted.

"I was the first layman in such a role on the Roman Catholic payroll," says Bonisteel proudly. He began his major job as the Director of Broadcasting, National Radio Co-ordinator of Interchurch Broadcasting, in September 1967. And then, in that same month, the CBC approached him with an offer to host a new show called *Man Alive*. The first show went to air the next month.

"They wanted me as a layman, a broadcaster, and because I was nondenominational," he recalls, and they got all three for the price of one. For two years and a touch, from 1967 to 1970, it was Man Busy: Roy Bonisteel did both the interchurch work and *Man Alive*, both free-lance. But he finally resigned from the church-appointed job: "There was just too much to do on *Man Alive*," he confesses. "By 1970, it was already very popular, and it was a full-time job for me."

It was love at first work. "It's a *good* show, and the kind I always *wanted* to do," says Bonisteel. "Here was a show you could *really* get your teeth

"I said that I'd only work for them on a nondenominational basis"

The Bonisteel family at their farm near Trenton, Ontario (left to right): son-in-law Ken Grant, Roy with granddaughter Jessie Bonisteel, wife Jane, daughter-in-law Tracy Trottier, daughter Lesley Grant with her daughter Emily, and daughter Mandy Berkshaw with daughter Siobhan.

"I'd never interviewed a god before!"

into. It dug deeper, and covered the whole waterfront, from native people to Mother Teresa."

The same year that Roy Bonisteel decided to put all his hours and thoughts into his TV show, he also moved to his fifty-acre farm, where he soon had seven cows, twelve horses, pigs, chickens, "the whole works!" Today, it is animal-free, but bursting with everything else: he grows corn, 60,000 cabbages, "good broccoli," asparagus, raspberries, cherries, grapes. "It's a working farm," he says, "and I spend as much time as I can there."

Bonisteel lives there with his wife Jane, who manages Roy Bonisteel Communications Limited, the speeches, the book-writing, and his show duties. Living on a farm means that he can "have fifteen for dinner on Sunday," as he puts it. He sponsors a junior ball team, which means wienie roasts. And every fall there is a *Man Alive* party at his farm, when forty to forty-five people from the show drive out to Trenton to enjoy fresh corn on the cob, steaks from a local butcher, a live six-piece Dixieland band—"a wonderful feed!"

Living on a farm makes food a pleasure. "I make homemade sourdough bread, and I'm a good dessert-maker. I make gooseberry pie, and since I grow cherries, I just finished making four gallons of cherry wine." Not that the local restaurants are ignored: he loves the Waring House near Picton, Ontario ("a home-atmosphere restaurant"), and Alexander's, outside Trenton.

His favourite inverviews? The one with author Elie Wiesel, the survivor of the Holocaust, is "my all-time favourite; it moved a lot of people and me." And his talk with the Dalai Lama, because "I'd never interviewed a god before!" Of course, Jean Vanier has been on the show three or four times, and Bonisteel is pleased to count Mother Teresa as "a regular guest."

It all makes sense, really. A religious show, and a man with his hands deep in God's good earth. "I loved this area, growing up, and I wanted my kids to have the experience of growing up on a farm." As for *Man Alive*: "I could *never* go back to games or sports shows!" Nor would we want him to.

Sourdough Bread

Sourdough Starter

The original recipe for starter is simply 2 cups flour and 2 cups water. It is credited to both Columbus and the miners during the gold rush. In the case of Columbus, it is said that sea water seeped into the bags of flour. The cook had to use the "spoiled" flour to make bread and discovered it was delicious. The miners maintained that it was discovered because they had limited access to general stores, and they could always have the basis for biscuits on hand. They would make the biscuit dough and keep half behind to use as the basis for the next batch. Because of refrigeration, the "staying" power of sourdough is no longer its essential feature. I use it because of its marvelous taste.

Ingredients

1 pkge. active dry yeast	1 pkge.
2 cups warm water	500 mL
2 cups all-purpose white flour	500 mL

Instructions

Dissolve yeast in the warm water in a stone jar or crock. Stir in flour. Place mixture in a warm place for 3 or 4 days, or until it is bubbly and smells sour. Then refrigerate it. When you use the starter, replace with an equal amount of both flour and water. If following the recipe above, replace with 1 cup (250 mL) flour and 1 cup (250 mL) water.

Wine

During preparation of Sourdough Starter, sip a glass of crisp, dry Manzanilla—in memory of Columbus who began his voyage to the New World from the sherry-producing region of Spain.

Sourdough Bread Ingredients

1 pkge. active dry yeast	1 pkge.
2 cups warm water	500 mL
1 cup sourdough starter	250 mL
2 cups all-purpose flour	500 mL
2 tbsp. honey	30 mL
1 tsp. salt	5 mL
3 tbsp. margarine, melted	45 mL
3–4 cups all-purpose white flour	750 mL –1 L
1 tbsp. butter, melted	15 mL

Instructions

These ingredients form the basis of sourdough bread; however, you can add cheese, eggs, herbs, tomato, or pepperoni to make specialty breads. Dissolve yeast in warm water. Add sourdough starter and blend thoroughly. Mix in the 2 cups flour. Add honey, salt, and margarine. Mix well. Add remaining flour until a soft dough has formed. Knead mixture on floured surface for about 10 minutes, or until folds form in dough ball. Place ball in a greased bowl. Grease the top and cover. Let it rise until doubled in bulk (about 1 hour). Punch it down and knead for 2 minutes. Shape into loaves and place in greased pans. Let rise until the top of the loaf rises above the rim of the pan (about 1 hour). Place in cold oven. Set oven at 375°F (190°C) and bake for about 60 minutes or until done. You can usually tell when the bread is done by tapping the top. You should hear a hollow sound, or you can see if the bread separates easily from the sides of the pan. Remove loaves from pan. Cool on rack and brush the tops with melted butter.
Yields 3 Loaves

Beverage

Chilled buttermilk—or if you plan to use the loaves as doorstops, Bloody Marys decorated with celery sticks.

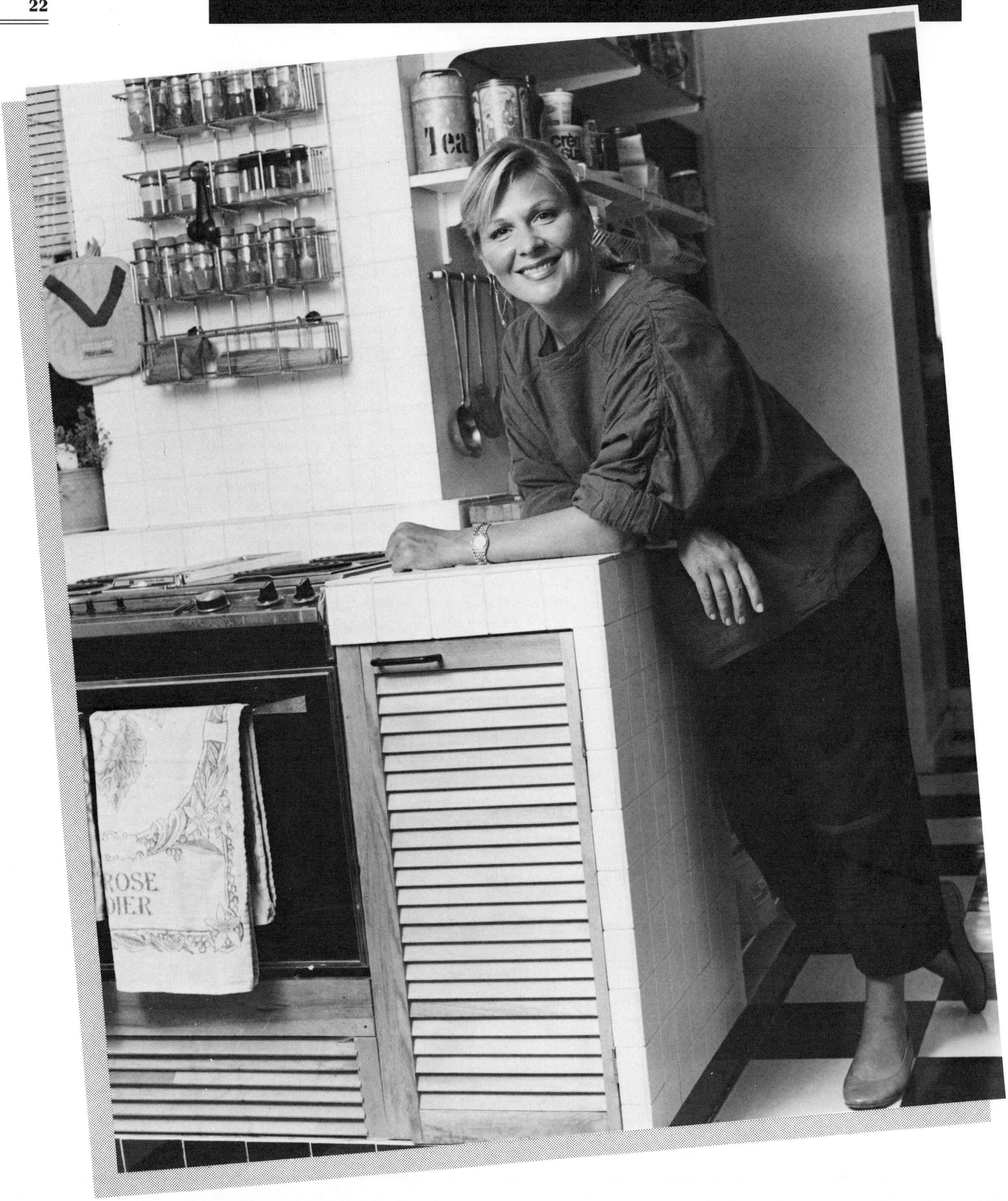
Tea
ROSE
DIER

Lally Cadeau

The star of Hangin' In *loves to travel and entertain friends at home*

*L*ally Cadeau is half French Canadian, but was raised in Ontario. Her mother was involved with Girl Guides and the IODE, and her father was the president of the Ontario Liberal Party. ("It was touted that he'd be premier of Ontario but he met an untimely death in 1954.")

Lally Cadeau was born in 1948 in the steel capital of Canada, Hamilton, Ontario, and was raised in nearby Burlington "when it was a little cow patch. Across the road was an orchard becoming a subdivision," and it was a "lovely childhood," what with all the property on the lake. After her father's death the teen-aged girl went off to various prep and Catholic schools in the United States before ending up at the exclusive all-girls Havergal in Toronto in her late teens. "But I was put back a year, and was getting 98s, and was dying to move on."

So she began to travel around the world—she still does, frequently—and never went to college, although there has been a lot of self-education since then. "I loved literature and English and language and history. If I hadn't had to contend with math and science, I could have been an extremely good college student."

It was out West—she lived seven years in Vancouver—that Lally Cadeau began her theatre career in 1972. She was twenty-four. "I started out at the Arts Club, then the Vancouver Playhouse, then lunchtime theatres." And there was always more travelling, playing Nora in *A Doll's House* in Regina and Kate in *The Taming of the Shrew* in New Brunswick. "I had wonderful parts! I even played Lady Sneerwell!" She also worked on a number of new plays in Vancouver and did some radio and TV, but there was no hint, back then, that she would become almost a staple of Canadian situation comedy just a decade later.

Then came the Lennoxville Festival in Quebec for a few years, and Cadeau passed through Toronto. "I thought how much it had changed and how nice it would be to live there." And so she moved back to her native Hamilton in the summer of 1979.

And then all heaven broke loose; a part in *Harvest*, "a good *For the Record*"—for which she won the Best Newcomer to TV Award. (Working in Vancouver television doesn't count, one presumes.) Finally came the TV play that truly helped her to be discovered: *You've Come a Long Way, Katie*," which won a number of awards.

"I had wonderful parts! I even played Lady Sneerwell!"

"Then Jack [Humphrey, the man who also produced, with Louis Del Grande, *King of Kensington*] offered me a series. I thought it would go for ten weeks. We're now into our fifth season! It's all been perfect." Indeed it has. Because Lally Cadeau has *still* been able to find the time to do theatre in between the tapings of *Hangin' In*. She even took a three-week immersion course in French (finally catching up to that name of hers) and found it "thrilling to do a play in French by Michel Tremblay").

Off the stage, life is sweet as well. She has a thirteen-year-old daughter, Sara Brooke ("she's just lovely, very much her own person"), and she's had "a male friend" for the past six years.

Cadeau and friend entertain a lot—"we like it" —with one party around Christmas each year, when they "manage to fit around 150 into our house." They enjoy having friends bring their own favourite dishes, "including fabulous desserts and great casseroles and inventive things."

The travelling continues. "I'm really fond of Italian food, and went to Italy a few years ago. But I enjoy French cuisine as well, and spent a month in Italy, France, and Switzerland recently. Halfway through France, I began to crave Italian food!" Others might swoon over Roman ruins, but Cadeau revels over her discovery of Amarone, "a fabulous Italian wine! And I had my first experience with a really wonderful Sauterne, a Barsac, 1971. It was as if the heavens

> *"I used to fast long before it became popular to do so"*

had opened it up, to taste it! And a Chateau D'Yquem—wonderful!"

Not that everything translates well back into English. "I tried to re-create Venetian liver and onions for friends, and ended up with a huge soup pot one-quarter full of liver, and one and a half feet of onions. It was an enormous failure, but it was all eaten up!" Other fiascos have to do more with entertaining than with actual cooking. An extra person came to a party recently, and she had painted a chair for the occasion: "He walked out with black slats across his white pants!"

Favourite restaurants include Pronto and Joe Allen in Toronto, and all the love for food takes its toll: "Oh God, I watch my diet. I used to fast long before it became popular to do so. I tend to drink a great deal of water, but I never get down to the weight I should ideally be at. But I'm always conscious of water, fiber, and vitamins and balancing things out." It helps that Lally Cadeau is no snacker, preferring fresh fruit to chocolate.

She loves gardening and renovating and decorating of her house. On the surface, she seems a homebody, reading cookbooks, doing needlepoint, silkscreening—"the most domestic kinds of hobbies." But don't assume too soon. "Not that I *am* so domesticated," she leaps in. "I'd go to Tibet in a flash. But I *do* enjoy my home."

Behind it all, of course, is that rare thing which Lally Cadeau has, and which 95 percent of her fellow performers lack: a long-running TV series. "It's great to be able to work so constantly and have security, so that I can travel and do other plays."

That's far more than merely hanging in, as one can readily see.

VINTNERS' STOCK POT AND GOUGÈRE

This fabulous, filling soup is fun to serve and eat in Burgundian style with a hearty Burgundy. Serve the soup in big round bowls, into which the croutons are placed first. Bake the first Gougère during the last 60 minutes of the soup's cooking time, and have the second one ready to pop into the oven before you sit down. It'll be ready when your guests want more. You can follow it with a great chocolate mousse, brandy snaps, good strong coffee, and Marc de Bourgogne. What an evening!

INGREDIENTS

1 1/2 lbs. ham slice	750 g
1/2 lb. lean slab bacon	250 g
2 lbs. pork sausages	1 Kg
2 3/4 qts. water	2.5 L
2 medium-sized carrots	2
4 white turnips	4
1 large onion	1
6 leeks	6
1 small cabbage	1
6 small potatoes	6
1 cup fresh lima beans	250 mL
1 baguette, sliced and toasted for croutons	1

INSTRUCTIONS

Brown the ham slice, bacon, and pork sausages in a heavy soup pot. Drain off excess fat. Add the water and simmer the meat for 1 1/2 hours. Peel and coarsely chop carrots, turnips, and onion. Wash and slice leeks. Remove the hard core, stem, and limp outer leaves from the cabbage and cut it into 4 wedges. Add these vegetables to the soup and cook until they are partially softened. Peel the potatoes and cut them into eighths. Add them with the lima beans to the soup. Add more water if necessary, and cook until the meat and vegetables are tender. Remove meat and cut into serving pieces. Arrange the sliced meat and cabbage on a serving platter. Serve with the soup. Guests may add the meat to the soup or eat it separately with Dijon mustard.
Serves 8

WINE

A two-fisted red wine is needed to stand up to this powerful dish. Try Côtes du Rhone-Villages, California Zinfandel, or a Portuguese Dão.

GOUGÈRE

INGREDIENTS

1/3 cup butter	75 mL
1 cup milk	250 mL
1/4 tsp. salt	1 mL
1 cup all-purpose flour, sifted	250 mL
4 large eggs	4
1 tbsp. whipping cream	15 mL
1/2 cup Swiss or Gruyère cheese, shredded	125 mL
A pinch dry mustard	a pinch
3 tbsp. Swiss or Gruyère cheese, diced	45 mL

INSTRUCTIONS

Heat butter and milk in a large saucepan over a low flame. When butter melts, blend in salt and flour, stirring constantly and energetically until mixture comes away from the side of the pan. Beat one egg at a time into the dough. Remove the pan from the stove after adding each egg so that the dough doesn't burn, beating constantly while on and off the stove. Stir in cream, shredded cheese, and mustard. Mound the mixture on a greased 10-inch (25-cm) pie plate. Garnish the top with the diced cheese and bake in a preheated 375°F (190°C) oven. After 30 minutes, turn the heat down to 350°F (180°C) and bake 10 minutes longer (40 minutes in all). Serve hot with lots of butter. (We've loved it with Dijon mustard on it as well.)
Serves 6–8

WINE

This Burgundian dish calls for a white wine of the region—Macon Blanc or better.

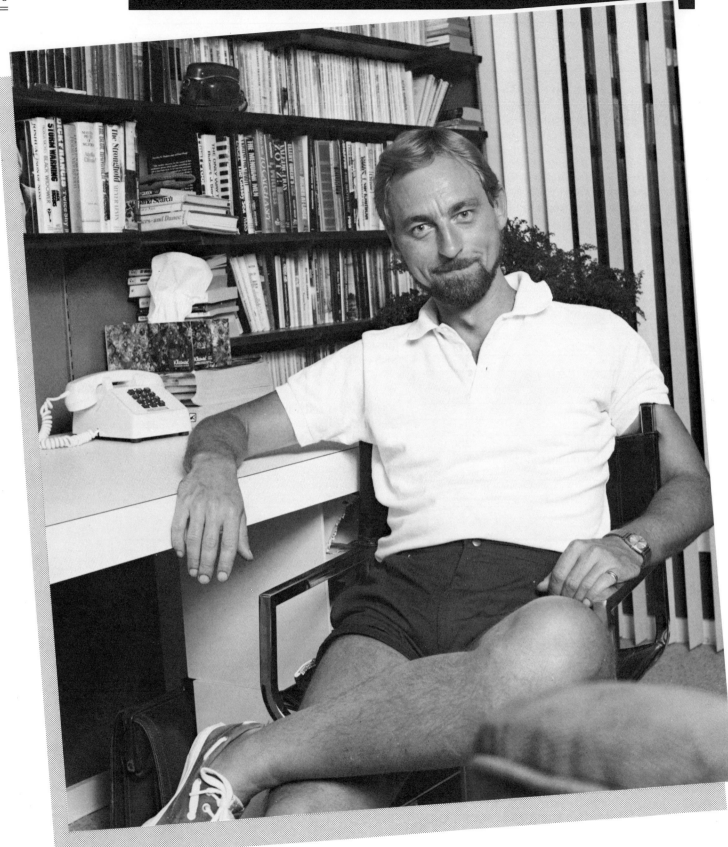

Terry Campbell

This busy radio host finds time to entertain friends for brunch

Terry Campbell has a problem that most of us would just love to suffer from: he has trouble keeping weight *on*. "I tend to run ten pounds under," he says. And if we eat the salmon mousse for which he so kindly sent along a recipe, we'll probably be another ten pounds *over*.

His weight level can't be *all* credited to a twenty-hour-a-week schedule on CBC Stereo, from 6 A.M. to 10 A.M. Monday through Friday, plus many, many more hours of research, interviews, selection of music, pre-tapings, etc., etc., etc. A good metabolism probably helps.

And so has a rather complex, peripatetic, cross-country jumping from job to job that would keep Elizabeth Taylor slim. Terry Campbell's origins are less cosmopolitan than one might expect, but just as intellectual, considering the musical and critical literacy he brings to his show. He was born in Portage La Prairie, about fifty miles west of Winnipeg, on March 19, 1947, to a businessman father and a teacher-and-school-principal mother. He ended up at the University of Manitoba in Winnipeg, "bouncing around" in Canadian history, political science, and English.

But before all that came the special moment in the lives of so many of us: the proverbial Big Break. In typically Canadian fashion—for how Big can a Break be in a Small Town?—it came almost sideways, and in a quiet manner. The high school principal in Portage La Prairie announced that the local station was looking for someone to do the swing shift for a buck an hour."

Campbell was fifteen, and the bug soon bit, to coin an old phrase. He did weekend work in seven-hour shifts, playing everything from barbershop quartets and pipe music to big band, country, folk, and rock. Hardly the stuff of *Stereo Morning* two decades later, but certainly knock-out experience. Then he worked at a station in Brandon, doing TV as well as radio (CKX), and later took the job of all-night DJ at a rock station (CKRC). He worked right through university—he never finished the degree—putting in a six-day week for $250 a month.

His first brush with the CBC, as a summer casual, came in 1967 in Winnipeg, at $367 a month. "That was a big jump!" he chuckles today. That was the year of the Pan Am games, when they were hiring a lot of casuals: "In one week of a forty-hour shift, I had a single ten-second TV break and one thirty-second radio weather break!"

But not for long. "All hell broke loose" when all staffers went on holiday, and Campbell found himself doing a 6-to-9 A.M. disc show, then reading a newscast to Saskatchewan from 9 to 9:10 A.M., followed by FM broadcasting until noon, "picking all the music." It was in the days before "information radio," with all the interviews, weather, sports, and so forth.

"The local station was looking for someone to do the swing shift for a buck an hour"

The next decade—until he came to Toronto and replaced Eric Friesen on what would eventually be called *Stereo Morning* in October of 1978 —reads like a blur of broadcasting activity: News director in Brandon. News, production, and writing for TV in that city. School broadcast producer for CBC. Producing the local equivalent of the Gerussi show: *David Brodie Today*. Producing the *Bruce Smith Show* in Toronto. Working on *Info Radio* back in Winnipeg. Producing and directing *Inside from the Outside* (with Barbara Hamilton and Max Ferguson, among others) back in Toronto. Producing and writing *Playdate*, which filled in for the Metropolitan Opera on Saturday afternoons. Staff announcing in Winnipeg. Producing *Info Radio* in Ottawa. Hosting the 4-to-6 P.M. show in Edmonton. Hosting the *Take 30* segments on Edmonton TV. Hosting the morning *Info Radio* in that city. Executive producer for music, variety, and drama for the Edmonton and Calgary radio stations of CBC.

Wouldn't *you* have trouble keeping *your* weight on, too? In the fall of 1984 he began his seventh season of *Stereo Morning*, rising at 4:30 A.M., guzzling coffee and puffing cigarettes, "speaking gently to the animals" (a Lhasa Apso dog named Archie and two cats named Bogart and Gabriella—all "its," alas), then cabbing to the old, dilapidated Toronto radio building and beginning the feed to Halifax, which, as any old radio hand knows, is one hour earlier than Toronto.

Despite his busy schedule, Terry Campbell enjoys having people over—but only once or twice a month. "Not as often as I like," he says, "but I value my private time. With the rigours of the job, time becomes more valuable." And he *does* love to cook, as you can see by the recipes he's offering below. He loves to use a lot of ginger and garlic in his Chinese cooking, enjoys Scotch in the winter, vodka in the summer, and wine all year round.

But it's rough having to spin beautiful music all the time. Notes Campbell, "I've always had the idea that if you want listeners, give muffin recipes over the radio. My greatest frustration is, I've never had the opportunity to do any cooking on the air."

But there are pleasures to make up for the lack. Meals at the old Owl's Nest in the Calgary Inn, at The Church in Stratford, Ontario, and at Ristorante San Lorenzo in downtown Toronto, a fine Italian eatery.

Not surprisingly, perhaps, he tends to veer away from the music he works eight hours a day with, enjoying Thelonius Monk, "early Miles Davis," Bobby Short, and what they call A/C (adult contemporary) listening stations. After the sort of far-flung broadcasting career he has managed to squeeze into the last twenty-odd years, it's more surprising that he didn't end up as a conductor on a CN train—and a lot less skinny.

SALMON MOUSSE

I like brunches and weekends, and with the hours I keep, early afternoon is the perfect time to entertain. I don't nod off during the appetizer, and I don't start the pointed watch-gazing to remind guests that some of us have to get up at 4:30 Monday mornings.

Here's a typical brunch at my house. It's typical because it can be made ahead of time (days, even), is easy to serve, and leaves the host time to get some of the good wine before the screw-top bottles come out. I serve a cold salmon mousse with a cucumber dressing, a big green salad, fresh rolls, and a raspberry creme soufflé. It's rich, but that's typical, too.

INGREDIENTS

1 envelope unflavoured gelatin	1
1/4 cup cold water	50 mL
1/2 cup boiling water	125 mL
1/2 cup very good mayonnaise	125 mL
1 tbsp. lemon juice	15 mL
1 tbsp. onion, finely grated	15 mL
Dash of Tabasco	a dash
1/2 tsp. sweet paprika	2 mL
2 tbsp. (or more, to taste) fresh dill, finely chopped	30 mL
2 cups fresh salmon, finely flaked (The same amount of skinned and boned canned red salmon works just as well, and is a lot easier.)	500 mL
1 cup whipping cream	250 mL

INSTRUCTIONS

Soften gelatin in cold water in a large bowl. Stir in the boiling water and whisk slowly until dissolved. Let cool to room temperature. Whisk in mayonnaise, lemon juice, onion, Tabasco, paprika, and dill. Blend completely and refrigerate for about 20 minutes. Mixture should thicken slightly. Fold in the salmon. In a separate bowl or food processor, whip the cream until it peaks. Fold gently into the salmon mixture. Transfer mixture into a clean bowl or mould (6 cup [1.5 L] size), cover, and chill for at least 4 hours. Unmould and decorate with watercress and serve with cucumber dressing.
Serves 6

CUCUMBER DRESSING

INGREDIENTS

1/2 cup plain yogurt	125 mL
1/4 cup sour cream	50 mL
1/4 cup green onion, finely chopped	50 mL
Pinch of salt (optional)	a pinch
1 small cucumber, peeled, seeded, and finely diced	1

INSTRUCTIONS

Combine all ingredients and pour over salmon mousse or, if desired, serve on the side.
Serves 6

WINE

White Burgundy or Pouilly Fumé from the Loire. For the connoisseur who actually listens to the *Arts News* and understands it, a German Riesling Spätlese.

Ernie Coombs

Mr. Dressup eats "anything that swims or crawls, except sea urchins!"

Shakespeare wrote that a tide, when "taken at the flood," can change one's life forever. In the case of Ernie Coombs, the mild-mannered man who has been entertaining Canadian children as Mr. Dressup since the mid-'60s, the Great Moment had to do with "pretty ingenues." You see, Coombs had studied commercial art in Boston (he was born in Lewiston, Maine, on November 26, 1927), but one summer he was "happily sidetracked" at his summer cottage. He loved to look at the attractive young actresses at a nearby summer theatre, got into painting scenery, and ended up in scenery design "without ever studying it."

"I decided that I liked theatre more than commercial art," he says today in his home in suburban Toronto. He did a few walk-ons, eventually worked on television in Pittsburgh, and came up to Canada with Fred Rogers (of *Mr. Rogers' Neighborhood* fame) as a puppeteer. "I came up with my dog, wife, and baby daughter; Fred came up with his son."

The CBC was beginning a new show called *Butternut Square* in 1964, and Ernie Coombs figured that his work in this country would last a few years. But it developed into *Mr. Dressup*, and here he is, two decades later, all thanks to those attractive young summer stock actresses in Maine.

Coombs has been married since 1962, and has two children, Cathie (twenty-two) and Chris (nineteen). His wife Lynn runs a day-care centre in Scarborough, Ontario. Cathie is studying early childhood education, while Chris is attending the American Academy of Dramatic Arts in Pasadena, suggesting that both offspring have been bitten by the child-oriented/performing bug of their famous father.

It wasn't all smooth sailing for Mr. Dressup. About two and a half years after *Butternut Square* began, funds were being shifted into covering Expo, and the show was about to be axed. But because "they got a lot of mail," the CBC decided to keep the show but reduce it in scope and size. Coombs, the second principal character, found himself as the star of a new show, along with his puppets. And, somewhat comically, *Mr. Dressup* was created because "the producer convinced the CBC that it was cheaper to produce my show than to buy films to fill the time slot."

> *"I decided that I liked theatre more than commercial art"*

Ernie Coombs and son Chris put their heads together over the dinner menu.

There are food stories related to the show, as one might imagine. Such as the time Coombs cut open an apple to show its seeds, and he couldn't find any. Or the other time he was supposed to make bread on the program. "The dough got sticky and stuck to my hand. And because of the time element of *Mr. Dressup*, going live-to-tape, with little editing, I just had to do the entire show with masses of dough all over my hands."

Ernie Coombs and his wife are as quiet off the set as one might imagine, on the basis of the sweet, quiet character he plays *on* the air. "We don't entertain; we're kind of reclusive," he admits. "I like to go home and recline with a good book."

Surprisingly, Coombs is not very organized. "If the kids only knew!" he cracks. Their house still isn't finished, and they've been living in it for fifteen years. He likes to play with cars; in fact they have five. Two are old English sports cars, including a 1932 Auburn ("the first car I ever owned"), which he is restoring "very, very slowly. It's a lovely old car," he says fondly.

Mr. Dressup is Mr. Paintup, off camera. He does watercolours, going off to his native Maine each summer to paint lighthouses, spruces, and rocks. He enjoys cooking, but nothing fancy: "I throw a lot of stuff into a salad, and sometimes it's a disaster. I don't go by the book very much." A lifelong seafood fan—"coming from Maine, it's no surprise"—he'll devour anything "that swims or crawls, except sea urchins." He once worked in a sardine factory, and still loves the things.

Both Coombs and his wife quit smoking last spring ("if one quits, the other has to"), but he refused to give up his coffee. "I like it very strong. I'll drink a whole pot and get the heebie-jeebies." Favourite restaurants include such Toronto mainstays as Parkes and Cibo, the latter near Studio 4, where he tapes his show.

There have been three *Mr. Dressup* record albums, which sell well at his many stage appearances across the country. "We travel in a motor home: me, a musician, and my tickle trunk." And when not taping or doing live performances, there is always skiing and golf, depending upon the season. Formal exercise is no great concern, since Coombs often forgets to eat breakfast or lunch, avoids salt, and does "a lot of running around." As he puts it, "climbing in and out of a low-slung sports car is enough exercise!"

It's all kind of strange, really, Ernie Coombs never had a steady job: until his TV character came along, he bounced from scene-designing to puppeteering to truck-lettering. "Lynn and I were discussing it just the other day: what would have happened if I'd gone back to the States, as Fred Rogers did? If I'd planned a career, Lord knows *what* would have happened. I'm delighted it's worked out this way!"

So are two generations of Canadians.

PASTA WITH CLAM SAUCE

INGREDIENTS

¹/₄ cup olive oil	50 mL
1 medium clove garlic, chopped	1
1 small onion, chopped	1
¹/₂ green pepper, chopped	¹/₂
2 5-oz. cans baby clams, minced	2 142-g cans
Parsley, chopped	
Optional: white wine, grated Romano cheese	
Pasta	

INSTRUCTIONS

Sauté garlic in olive oil until dark brown, then discard. Add green pepper and onion to oil, and sauté until soft. Toss in a splash or two of white wine, then add the clams and their broth. When the sauce is thoroughly heated, scatter the chopped parsley onto it, and serve over your favourite pasta. Grated cheese may be added at this point.
Serves 4

WINE

Make sure the children are in bed, then open a bottle of Soave or dry Orvieto.

MARINATED MACKEREL

I got this recipe from Mrs. Ruth Sheppard of Brudenell Resort, Prince Edward Island.

INGREDIENTS

5 lbs. mackerel	2.5 Kg
1 cup water	250 mL
2 tbsp. salt	30 mL
3 cups white vinegar	750 mL
4 bay leaves	4
Marinade:	
2 tbsp. peppercorns	30 mL
12 whole cloves	12
1 tsp. cinnamon	5 mL
1 tsp. ginger	5 mL
1 tbsp. garlic salt	15 mL
1 large onion, cut in rings	1
¹/₄ cup soy sauce	50 mL
2 cups brown sugar	500 mL
¹/₂ cup salad oil	125 mL

INSTRUCTIONS

Poach the mackerel in water, salt, vinegar, and bay leaves. Mix together the remaining ingredients for the marinade. Bring to a full boil, and pour over the poached mackerel. May be put in jars. Kept refrigerated, it's good for a year or so.

BEVERAGE

Iced vodka or Danish akvavit in shot glasses. Keep the bottle in the freezer to get as cold as possible (40 percent alcohol by volume will not freeze in there).

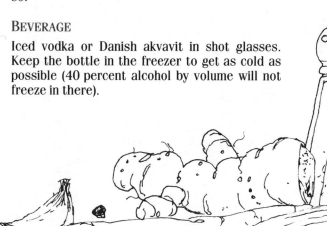

Sandy Cushon

"Take five plump field mice, add a pinch of salt..."

*U*nlike many of the men and women in this book who almost fell into broadcasting or performing, Sandy Cushon was almost to the manor (and manner) born. For what could be more logical than a young man, born on a family farm in Oxbow, Saskatchewan (on February 8, 1946), ending up as the host of an agricultural TV show?

Not that it was a straight journey from A to B. Cushon went to the proverbial one-room school-house in that small town of about a thousand, tucked away in the southeast corner of the province, and then went east to Carleton University in Ottawa, from 1965 to 1970, obtaining a degree in political science and journalism.

And it was political writing he was interested in, not journalism. He had *wanted* to go off to write for *The Wall Street Journal*, but ended up working for the Ontario Ministry of Agriculture in Guelph, Ontario, as an information officer and press writer. (You can take the boy out of the country, but you can't take the country, etc.) As he puts it, "I had lots of debts from school," and wanted to earn some money.

Cushon was in Guelph two years to the day, from late 1970 to 1972, when he joined *Radio Noon* in Toronto as their agriculture commentator. "It was the Golden Age of *Radio Noon*," recalls Cushon. "Arthur Black was on the show, Joan Watson was doing consumer items, and Al Maitland was the host."

The only catch was that Sandy Cushon may have known where little piggies came from but he had no broadcasting experience whatsoever. "I lost fifteen pounds in the first month I was on the air!" he exclaims. "I was scared out of my mind."

But it all worked out for the best, as the hundreds of thousands of fans of *Country Canada* have known for the past decade. Cushon was with *Radio Noon* for a year and a half, leaving in July 1974 to move to Winnipeg, to work on a TV series called *Points West*. He worked there for a year, "doing agricultural input," before returning to Toronto, first as a commentator and soon the host of *Country Canada*.

Cushon is proud of the show. "It's the CBC's longest-running serious program: October of 1984 marked thirty years. It's been on the air longer than *anything* with the exception of news and hockey!"

Over the years, the show has changed from being "strictly for farmers and rural audiences" to a far broader coverage of food and food production. Indeed, July 1984 saw Cushon doing an item in Toronto on pasta with the Food Editor of *Chatelaine*. "The pasta revolution falls within our borders now," he adds.

And those borders are changing in other ways as well. In the summer of 1984 *Country Canada* moved lock, stock, and host out to Winnipeg. For many, the move to a small prairie city from big urban Toronto would be earth-shattering, but one must not forget Cushon's prairie origins. "It's tough to leave friends and places that I've grown to like. But I'm a prairie boy at heart, and it's nice to be close to my family again." (His parents and two brothers still farm the thirteen hundred acres outside Oxbow.)

It's not easy being a host of a show that leaps from pasta to biotechnology to politics to the crow rate to the world of the farmer. "We see the insides of a lot of aircraft and hotel rooms," admits Cushon, hinting that those account for, at

"The pasta revolution falls within our borders now"

his passion for food. Not to mention "an access to the freshest foodstuffs you can get!"

Cushon's tastes are fairly eclectic. "I like Greek and Chinese and Italian cooking…I *like* food! *Good* food!" Beer is another pleasure: "I drink beers from fifty to sixty different countries." And then there are the duties that come with being a host of a show like *Country Canada*, such as his having to become "one of the few people on the face of the earth to eat a roasted worm on camera."

I'd better explain. A few years ago they did an item on a woman in Stratford who raised worms for the fish-bait trade. The woman roasted a few to check the protein quality of the little things, and Cushon was somehow cowed into eating one. "I didn't chuck my cookies," he states poetically, "but I didn't eat more than one either!"

However, he's eaten raw mussels in conjunction with a story down in P.E.I. ("they're better when cooked"), and he's eaten moose meat as well—"but most people have," he insists. Hopefully, "most" have not suffered like Sandy Cushon did. It appears that he "got a bit of the end piece, so I was in the embarrassing situation of deciding whether to chew on it for fifteen minutes, or spit it out." You'll have to guess what he ended up doing.

Unlike most in this crazy business, Sandy Cushon is a vehement nonsmoker, shaken at having moved from a group of co-workers in Toronto, where only one smoked, to a new situation in Winnipeg where nearly everyone does. And he misses such wonderful Toronto restaurants as Il Focolare on St. Clair West and Casa Abril Em Portugal in Kensington Market.

Now his goal "is to discover Winnipeg" once again. And there's one consoling thought. Winnipeg is a lot closer to the best eatery in the country. As Cushon puts it, "In Oxbow, I recommend my mother's cooking, if you can wangle an invitation!"

"I was one of the few people on the face of the earth to eat a roasted worm on camera"

least partially, the fact that he has never been married. But life has been good, and he gets a lot of assistance in occasional entertaining "from my lady friend."

Cushon insists that "there are very, *very* good cooks in rural areas," which might help to explain

SASKATCHEWAN OLD-FASHIONED SASKATOON PIE

This is my mother's recipe, and probably at the top of the list as far as desserts are concerned. The first question anyone asks is: "What is a 'saskatoon'?" Well, in addition to being the second largest city in Saskatchewan, it's also a small delicious berry—not unlike a blueberry in appearance, but darker and with a distinctive taste all its own. By and large it grows wild, although there have been some commercial plantings in recent years, primarily in Alberta.

So, when seeking these elusive wild saskatoons, you must either purchase them from someone who has picked them, or—horror of horrors—you'll have to pick them yourself. (I recall my mother preserving upward of 100 quarts in a year, which is a considerable amount of picking.) They grow along the coulees and ravines of the prairies, but there's no guarantee of a crop from one year to the next.

One of the occupational hazards of picking saskatoons—apart from sunstroke and general physical malaise—is woodticks, little creepy crawlies that are none too pleasant. So, after a day of picking, the trick is to spend time examining oneself for any of the little critters that may have attached themselves in the interim. One final note: apparently, the Plains Indians used to pound saskatoons into their pemmican to make it more palatable.

INGREDIENTS

Pastry for a 9-in. (23-cm) double crust pie	
4 cups saskatoons	1 L
2 tbsp. water	30 mL
2 tbsp. lemon juice	30 mL
3/4 cup sugar	175 mL
1 1/2 tbsp. quick-cooking tapioca	25 mL
1 tbsp. butter or margarine	15 mL

INSTRUCTIONS

Simmer berries, water, and lemon juice over low heat, covered, for 3 or 4 minutes. Remove from heat and stir in sugar, tapioca, and butter. Cool and pour into pastry-lined pie plate. Cover with top crust; brush with milk and sugar if desired. Bake at 450°F (220°C) for 15 minutes. Reduce heat to 350°F (180°C) and bake 30–35 minutes longer. Reduce heat by 25° if using glass pie plate.
Serves 7

WINE

Since Saskatchewan is not noted as a grape-growing province, choose a sweet Vouvray from the Loire, Auslese quality German wine, or Late Harvest Californian Riesling.

FIELD MOUSE CASSEROLE

This recipe is courtesy my aunt in Winnipeg. It was given to her by a friend who found it in a pioneer cookbook from the mid-1800s in the United States. It tastes great.

INGREDIENTS

5 fat field mice	5
1 cup macaroni	250 mL
1/2 medium onion, sliced	1/2
1 19-oz. can tomatoes	1 540-mL can
1 cup cracker crumbs	250 mL
Salt and pepper	
Butter	

INSTRUCTIONS

Boil macaroni 10 minutes. Drain. Fry field mice until browned. In greased casserole, put in a layer of macaroni. Add onions, half of the tomatoes, salt, and pepper. Add field mice. Cover with remaining macaroni and tomatoes. Sprinkle top with cracker crumbs seasoned with salt, pepper, and butter. Bake at 350°F (180°C) 20 minutes or more.
Note: In cold or rainy weather when field mice are hard to find, the cook may substitute sausages.
Serves 4

WINE

Don't tell your guests what they're eating, or see how they run. If your cat joins you, a saucer of milk. Otherwise, any basic red mouse wine.

Warren Davis

Here's a radio host who shares the cooking duties with his wife

Warren Davis, one of the most respected and successful radio hosts in Canadian history, seems to have everything going for him: a wife of over thirty-four years, three attractive children (ranging from twenty-six to thirty-one) ("one of each," he says, insisting that *he* created that line before Victor Borge), and a very, very busy career.

But *one* mistake stands out in his three-plus decades of work on CBC. "It took three days for them to talk me into it" he recalls—the "them" being Knowlton Nash and Joe Schlesinger. "I knew as soon as I took it, it was a mistake, and I wrote my first letter of resignation after three months."

As you may have guessed by now, Davis is referring to the time he "let the ———— talk me into doing *The National*." No offence, Knowlton, but back then, they weren't allowed to do much more than *read* the news, and Warren Davis was interested in doing *far* more than *that*. (He stayed for one year and then quit.)

There haven't been any other mistakes that come to mind, at least on Warren Davis's part. (He still remembers with joy when a newspaper dug up his photograph at the time Bill Davis was about to move into politics, and ran a headline over it: "W. DAVIS TO RUN FOR THE CONSERVATIVES.")

W. (as in Warren) Davis was born in Peterborough, Ontario, on November 12, 1926, when his parents drove in from their small town to have him born in a hospital. His father died when he was only eight months old, and his mother moved to Toronto with him and his older sister. After he finished high school in Toronto he was volunteering on a radio show at the old CHUM station when the program director invited him to be an announcer. She then phoned up her friend, Lorne Greene, who was running his own Academy of Radio Arts on Jarvis Street, and the young boy studied there, two mornings a week, with the future Pa Cartwright, in 1951–52.

Warren Davis and wife Janice in their family home.

Shortly thereafter, Davis began at CBC in a wonderfully round-about fashion. He had been working as an advertising salesman for the Toronto *Telegram* in 1949, then moved up to Kenora, Ontario, to be both an ad salesman and a part-time announcer for a private station, CJRL. The station manager who had auditioned him for the job was George McLean, better known today as the reader of the weekend *National*. (You can't escape the past, can you?)

But most people with thirty-plus years at the CBC have similar tales. For example, Davis was soon confronted with a choice: accept a job in Windsor or Winnipeg. "Having spent one winter out west, I chose Windsor." He was there two and a half years, and who was another one-third

"Having spent one winter out West, I chose Windsor"

of the announce staff at CBE? Why, Lloyd Robertson, naturally.

Windsor was meaningful in another way. As he started the job as full-time announcer, he told everyone that he was called "Bill" Warren Davis. "Warren is a better name," was the reply. "So I switched over to a new city, new job, new friends, and a new name."

CBC job and location changes came fast and furiously. Davis was in Windsor from 1953 to 1955. Then he was transferred to Winnipeg, where he spent seven very happy years ("I *loved* that city!") doing all kinds of TV and radio, from being the host of the supper-hour TV show (*Spotlight*) to hosting a series of music shows (*Music Break*). In 1963 it was back to Toronto for good, in both meanings of the word. (He had done a few little theatre productions in Winnipeg—"strictly amateur"—but they must have taken, professionally. His part in the CBC-TV film *Drying Up the Streets* was powerfully understated.) Davis replaced Elwood Glover on holidays for a number of years. He was the announcer and on-camera interviewer for *This Hour Has Seven Days*. He hosted *TBA*, the supper-hour info show, later changed to *The Day It Is* on weekday TV, and *The Way It Is* on Sundays. He did a panel program series, *What on Earth?* and then spent a year reading *The National*. And did I remember to mention his hosting the first year of *Reach for the Top*, back in Winnipeg?

The radio shows have been almost nonstop. Warren Davis chuckles about how, for many of the last few years, the CBC schedule has read: "3 to 5:30 P.M., Sundays, *Live from Roy Thomson Hall*, with your host, Warren Davis"; "8 to 9 P.M., Sundays, *Celebration*, with your hosts Bronwyn Drainie and Warren Davis"; "9 to 11 P.M., *Two New Hours*, with your host, Warren Davis."

But with *Celebration* down to only six months a year, it's a bit calmer. "The schedule *did* look silly for a while, there." Silly, maybe. But busy, most assuredly. From Christmas 1983 to early June 1984 Davis had not a single weekend off. And, in the summer of 1984 he had the "delightful" *Morningside* job.

Davis shares the cooking duties approximately fifty-fifty with his wife Janice, who is the secretary to the dean of the Faculty of Education at the University of Toronto. He loves to eat, and will eat everything, with the exception of buttered parsnips. "Wrap them in pastry and I'll eat that, too!" He's a rye-and-water-in-winter and gin-and-tonic-in-summer man. "Just ask Chris-

tos, the bartender at Jingles," Davis's favourite bar on Church Street in Toronto.

Warren Davis's true hobby is "reading, reading, reading," but he loves food enough to share not only recipes with us but a funny story from his honeymoon. "I read *The New Yorker*; I was a real sophisticate, back in 1950. And I noticed this strange food, available in Boston and New York." The "exotic" dish was called "pizza pie," and the new couple vowed to try it.

After completing a sumptuous meal at the French restaurant in Rockefeller Plaza, the Davises refused dessert—"we have other plans"— and headed off until they saw a restaurant advertising this romantic "pizza." They came in, sat down, and asked for two pieces of pizza pie.

"*Pieces?*" shouted the owner. "You know what a pizza pie is? *That* is a pizza pie!" he howled, pointing to this massive thing on a nearby table. Warren and Janice settled for a dish of spumoni!

"Wrap them in pastry and I'll eat that too!"

ANTIPASTO

INGREDIENTS

1 qt. cauliflower	1 L
1 qt. carrots	1 L
1 qt. silverskin onions (leave whole if small enough)	1 L
1 qt. celery	1 L
1 qt. red and green peppers, mixed	1 L
Pickling salt	
2 13-oz. cans tomato paste	2 369–mL cans
2 tsp. pickling spice	10 mL
1 cup salad oil	250 mL
1 qt. vinegar	1 L
1 cup brown sugar	250 mL
1 qt. string beans, split and chopped	1 L
1 qt. black and green olives	1 L
3 7½-oz. cans tuna	3 220-g cans
3 cans anchovies	3 50-g cans
5 chicken breasts, cooked and chopped	5
1 lb. mushrooms, chopped and fried in oil	500 g
1 qt. sweet mixed pickles, chopped	1 L

INSTRUCTIONS

Cut cauliflower, carrots, onions, celery, and red and green peppers into coarse chunks. Sprinkle with a handful of pickling salt, and let stand overnight. The next morning, rinse salt off thoroughly. Then bring tomato paste, pickling spice, oil, vinegar, and brown sugar to boiling point. Add chopped vegetables and simmer 15 minutes, stirring continuously. Add string beans and olives. Boil 5 minutes, then add tuna, anchovies, chicken breasts, mushrooms, and mixed pickles. Boil 3 minutes and bottle. Note that the mushrooms should be fried in salad oil because butter will congeal when cold. Store only in freezer.

WINE

Since everything is measured by the quart, do not confuse the issue by ordering a litre of wine. Choose a wine beloved by Corsican bandits or B.C. loggers—a rugged Greek red, or retsina for those who can stand it.

BUTTERMILK TEA BISCUITS

INGREDIENTS

2 cups all-purpose flour	500 mL
2 tsp. baking powder	10 mL
½ tsp. baking soda	2 mL
1 tsp. salt	5 mL
½ cup margarine	125 mL
¾–1 cup buttermilk	175–250 mL
½ cup cottage cheese or grated cheddar cheese	125 mL

INSTRUCTIONS

Mix baking powder, soda, and salt together with flour in a large bowl. Cut margarine into the dry mixture. Add buttermilk and, if desired, cheese. Knead the mixture 10 to 15 times on a floured board. Roll out and cut out. Or drop by large spoonfuls onto cookie sheet. Bake 10 to 12 minutes on an ungreased cookie sheet at 450°F (230°C). Cooking time will be longer if cheese is added.
Makes 12 biscuits

BEVERAGE

Tea or coffee. If entertaining in a CBC canteen, avoid the coffee and bring your own flask of tea.

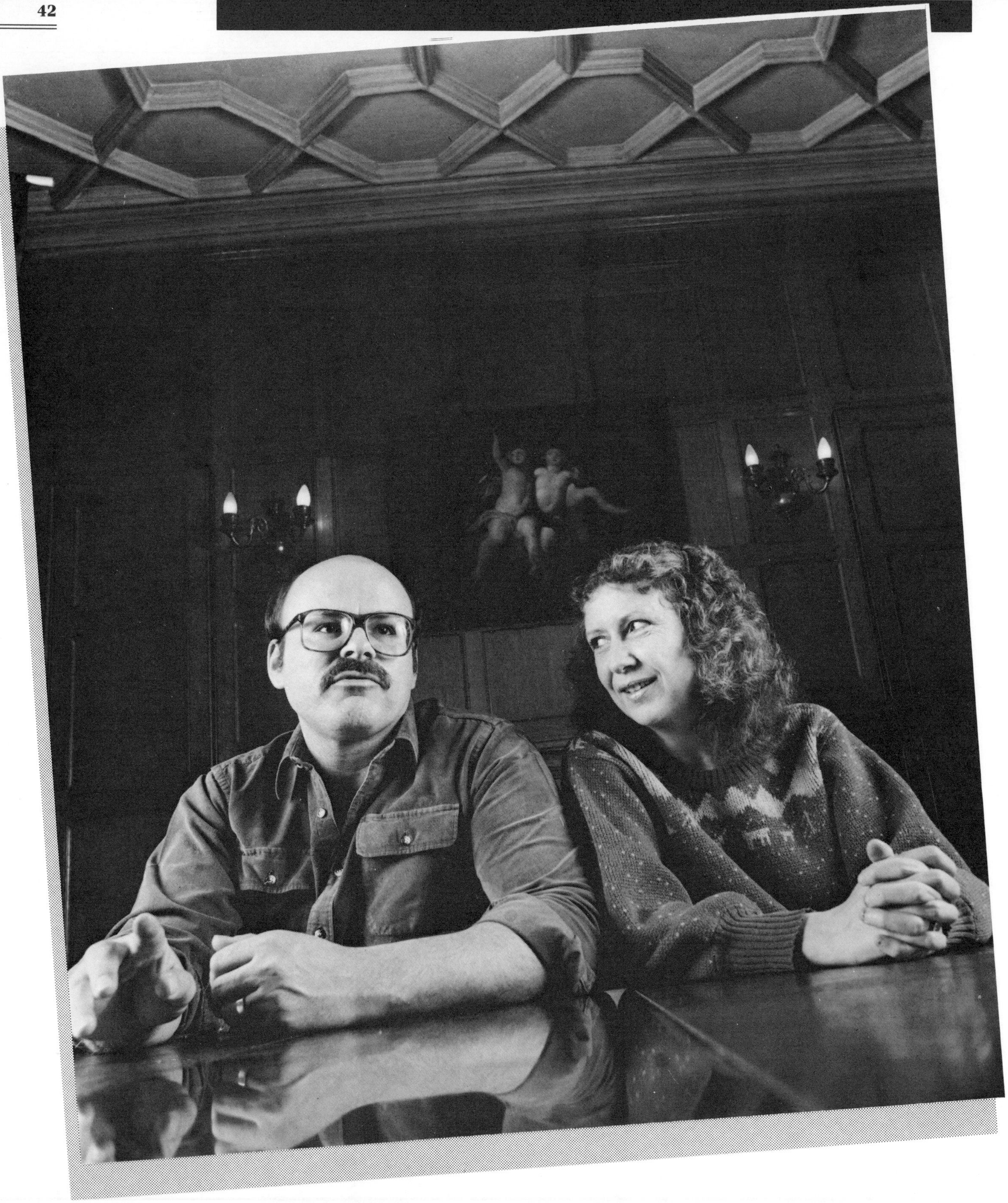

Louis Del Grande and Martha Gibson

After throwing parties for 200 people, it's no wonder this couple are Seeing Things

Louis Del Grande is not what you would call the ideal chef. He is, to be blunt, rather frenetic. "I am of the theory that if it says *two* spoonfuls of something, it will be better with four! If the recipe says a quarter of a cup of butter, I figure that it will be better with *half* a cup!" Bemoans his real-life wife Martha Gibson (who plays his estranged wife on the popular comedy/mystery series), "Louis really *is* a very unreliable cook. He's *too* creative with spices. Only he and I can end up eating it; it's always too spicy for the kids."

But look. The very freneticism, generosity, and creativity that make Louis Del Grande so dubious in the kitchen also make him wonderfully exciting as a writer, producer, and performer. And the over a million people in Canada who watch *Seeing Things* regularly, along with the tens of millions more who catch it on twenty-nine Public Broadcasting System affiliates in the States, and nearly three dozen foreign countries, can only cry "Amen."

Del Grande was born in 1943 in Union City, New Jersey, just across from that spectacular Manhattan skyline. He dropped out of school in Grade 10, worked as a male model for those crummy detective magazines of the 1950s, acted briefly off-Broadway, and ended up at the Stratford Festival in Ontario.

Martha Gibson, during the same period, was being born (she won't say when, but I am safe to say she's in her "late thirties") and raised in a tiny town in Illinois. She acted in summer stock, and ended up taking an acting course with one Louis Del Grande in New York City. The two married and moved up to Stratford in 1965, but Gibson's mom was so horrified by the match that she begged her daughter to leave the ne'er-do-well. She did, and that was that.

Or so it was in the mid-1960s. But this is, in a way, a kind of twisted fairy tale, so bear with me. Del Grande stayed in Canada, directing a workshop production at Stratford, and then became one of the leading lights of the exciting underground theatre scene of Toronto in the late '60s and early '70s, producing, directing, and even writing (one play lasted a glorious one night off-Broadway).

Martha Gibson, the future famous ex-wife of *Seeing Things* (and nonfamous ex-wife of the period I am describing), was down in Washington, D.C., working as a legal secretary and doing a bit of acting. Suddenly a phone call came from the ex in Canada: "I just had a leading actress take a walk from a play I'm directing. Could you come up and do it?"

You guessed it. Within days, they were back together again; within months, married a second time (will it happen that way in future *Seeing Things* shows, one wonders?), and now have three children ("great cooks!" exclaims Del Grande), Phillip, twelve; Tina, eight; and Victoria, three. Then came the co-writing and co-producing of the highly successful situation comedy *King of Kensington* and, since 1981, his present monster hit, co-produced, co-written (but not co-starred) with David Barlow, his long-time writing partner.

The use of Martha Gibson as Del Grande's ex-wife on *Seeing Things* was *not* nepotism at all but

"There's hardly a cuisine I've had that Martha doesn't make comparably or better"

The couple enjoy such classy meals as take-out pizza from Bravo's ("pizza with Elwy Yost every Saturday night!" says Louis, referring to the popular double bills of great films on TVOntario each weekend). Young Lok (Chinese) and Masa (Japanese) are also favourites. But Louis Del Grande insists that "there's hardly a cuisine I've had that Martha doesn't make comparably or better. My wife is a brilliant cook!"

Alas, it shows. Del Grande has hit over 200 pounds now, and considering his obsessions with cashew nuts and pasta, it *can* be a problem. Indeed, food is a kind of magnificent obsession with him. "Next to my libido, which has waned, nothing can usurp the interest I have in what I'll eat when I get home at night." Del Grande has the unfortunate habit of calling up his wife and asking, "What's for dinner?" every day. She once lost her cool and yelled, "I'M NOT TELLING YOU!" and hung up.

Martha Gibson, in the meantime, is a coffee addict, a nonsmoker, and is "always on a diet" (although the need for it doesn't show). Her favourite food recollections refer to the time she made a cake for visiting family, and her dog "walked on it, squashed it, and ate it." And another time, Louis went to open the fridge door, and a huge cake (this one chocolate) "flipped out on the floor. It went *right over*," says Gibson.

But there are other hobbies besides eating and avoiding eating. Del Grande loves to read, listen to music, go to art galleries, and cater to (there's that food word again) a "dangerous interest in antiques." "I want my house to look like an old Charlie Chaplin movie with Oriental rugs," he says.

Since Louis Del Grande and Martha Gibson are both fine comic performers, the Chaplin image is apt. But there's one fear: Charlie Chaplin lived to a ripe old age. "My pants size has almost kept up with my age!" moans Del Grande. "Now it's only one size smaller. I'm scared of growing older."

Far more of us are scared that *Seeing Things* might ever stop being shown.

"My pants size has almost kept up with my age!"

an inspired recognition of her rightness for the part. Other writers on the show recall how panic-stricken Gibson was when she went in for the audition: "People will think it's because I'm Louis's wife! I'm so *nervous*!" She got the part, and deservedly so.

In their busy life Del Grande and Gibson *do* manage to entertain, and twice a year they cook for the entire crew of the hit show—"about 200 people!" says Martha Gibson. The first time she risked that, she did it all herself; the last time, she wisely got a caterer. "We used to entertain a *lot* before we got into the series," Gibson recalls; "one or two people a week for dinner."

TUNA CUTLETS

You may find it odd that I have not included any Italian recipes when they are my "specialty." However, I am a firm believer that you can't get any good recipes out of the Italian people. They cook by smell and taste and instinct. So, I believe that if you want to learn, you have to go straight into an Italian's kitchen and watch. When I first got married, my mother and father-in-law tried to give me recipes, but they were of the "you'll know" school of cooking. I would say, "But how long do I cook the sauce?" "Don't worry," they'd say, "you'll know when it's done!" "How much basil do I add?" "Oh, a little bit," they'd reply. "You'll know when it's enough!" I finally gave up in despair of ever being able to write down a recipe, went into their kitchen, and watched. I have now become a "you'll know" cook myself when it comes to Italian food.

I include this tuna cutlets recipe because it is nutritious, cheap, and kids love it! When I went home last summer, an old playmate reappeared. He said, "Oh, Martha, remember those tuna fish things your mother used to make? Weren't they yummy?"

INGREDIENTS

3 tbsp. butter	45 mL
1/4 cup flour	50 mL
1 cup milk	250 mL
1 7-oz. can tuna, drained and flaked	1 189-g can
1/2 cup soft breadcrumbs	125 mL
1/2 tsp. onion, grated	2 mL
1/2 tsp. salt	2 mL
1/4 tsp. paprika	1 mL
1/2 tsp. Worcestershire sauce	2 mL
1 egg, beaten	1
Extra breadcrumbs	

INSTRUCTIONS

Make a white sauce by combining butter, flour, and milk. Add tuna, breadcrumbs, onion, salt, paprika, and Worcestershire sauce. Cook 5 minutes after all ingredients have been added. Spread on a plate to cool. Shape into small cutlets. Roll in crumbs, then egg, then crumbs. Brown in hot fat. Serve with creole sauce.

CREOLE SAUCE

INGREDIENTS

1/4 cup onions, chopped	50 mL
1/4 cup green pepper, chopped	50 mL
2 tbsp. salad oil	30 mL
1 7 1/2-oz. can tomato sauce	1 213-mL can
2 tbsp. pimento, chopped	30 mL
1 tsp. sugar	5 mL
1 tsp. salt	5 mL
1 tsp. pepper	5 mL

INSTRUCTIONS

Brown onions and green pepper in salad oil. Add remaining ingredients. Simmer 15 to 20 minutes.
Serves 3–4

WINE

A full-bodied dry white wine from Burgundy or Italy, California, or the antipodes. If you go with the spicy sauce you'll need a wine with residual sugar and high acidity, such as Californian Chenin Blanc, Ontario Vidal, or Rheinhessen Riesling.

Harry Elton

The man who gave us Coronation Street now gives us Steamed Lake Trout

*E*very book should contain a kind of secret, and here is this book's special one: there lurks a man in Ottawa, on the CBC announce staff, who is known and admired for his work on that city's morning radio show, *Cross Country Checkup*, and various music shows, who was directly responsible for one of the most popular *television* shows in British, and even global, history.

We are talking about Harry Elton. And the show we are referring to is *Coronation Street*, the much-loved program that has been running for a quarter-century. "I brought that show in," recalls Elton. "I found the writer, I worked with him on the first dozen scripts, and I put the entire unit together—the producer, the director, everyone."

Not that he has peaked, mind you. But *Coronation Street* certainly *was* (and *is*) a highlight of what has been (and is) a very fascinating, challenging, and creative life. As Harry Elton puts it, "I am a survivor, and I've survived in this business by recycling myself."

Let us cycle back with him. Harry Elton was born in Toronto on January 5, 1930, but even *that* would become extraordinary, in time. You see, he was the child of "a *very* late second marriage" for his father, who was the manager of the Toronto Symphony Orchestra. His father was dead by the time the child was three, and he was raised in a foster home in Thornhill, north of Toronto, until he was eight, at which time he was sent off to his mother in Detroit, where she was a teacher. He remained in that city from 1938 until 1956, taking pre-law at Wayne State University before switching to the theatre program there.

Elton never graduated, but he continued to be involved in related activities. He toured for a year, pulling strings for a marionette company, up and down the state of Michigan in 1950, and began doing free-lance commercials for WJBK, WXYZ, and WWJ while still in college. "I made my first appearance on TV in 1949 as the back end of a horse," he laughs, "and I've been fighting that casting ever since!"

Then began the first British stint. He went to the Royal Academy of Dramatic Arts in England for a year, during which point in time he decided that he "didn't want to be an actor, but wanted to be close to where the words were made."

So he returned to Detroit and resumed free-lance commercial announcing, and then became the floor director of WXYZ-TV, eventually directing Soupy Sales's lunchtime show. He remained at that popular Detroit station until 1956, when he returned to England and became a producer, then executive producer, of dramatic series and serials at Granada Television, one of the major private stations in the Motherland. There he was responsible for the astounding success, *Coronation Street*. As he modestly confesses, "It was one of *several* series I did, but that one clicked." Boy, did it!

Not that Harry Elton clicked when he came "to my home and native land in 1963," for the first time since he left it as a pre-adolescent, back in 1938. "They'd never heard of me, and it was cold!" His first job was washing floors in the Shell building; or, as he wittily puts it, "I started on the bottom floor of the oil industry." It was a long way downstairs from *Coronation Street*, he can tell you.

By that time Elton had married and had four children. (He is now divorced, the children are grown and live in Toronto and Ottawa, and they have provided him with grandchildren.) But those first few years in Canada were hardly easy. True, he got a "short, quick job at CBC drama, looking for writers." But he soon realized that all they wanted was "someone to say 'no,'" and he wasn't too happy saying "no" to the likes of Margaret Atwood.

"I made my first appearance on TV as the back end of a horse and I've been fighting that casting ever since!"

"I've done a lot in Canada," says Harry Elton. "Nothing as spectacular as *Coronation Street*, but many things that were very challenging and satisfying."

That's for sure. He went to CBC on a summer relief contract in 1971, then to permanent staff in Montreal in 1972; he did the evening TV hour and hosted *Cross Country Checkup* from 1973 to 1976 (a role later filled by Elizabeth Gray and Dennis Trudeau); after that, he was invited out to Calgary to be the director/manager of a new CBC station out there, and he stayed for three years.

Then, in 1979, Elton thought to himself, "Hey, I'll go back on the air! I had more *fun* on the air!" And so he went back to Ottawa and the announce staff, for which he hosted the *CBL Morning Show* in Ottawa from January 1979 until 1984, when he quit. "You get up at 4 A.M. for five years, and it's hard to think of something to say." He also hosted *Cross Country Checkup* again, in summer 1984.

Elton now hosts *Mostly Music*, CBC's orchestral concert program, aired on both AM and FM.

Away from the microphone, Harry Elton lives with Marguerite McDonald, the social-affairs reporter on CBC-TV. They entertain, but usually only a small number of people at a time, with Elton cooking Chinese food or a barbecue. "Marguerite cooks less; she's on the road a lot." Their favourite Ottawa restaurant for Italian food is La Gargotte. And their great escape is to go canoe-camping together, portaging for eight days, which they did in July 1984.

It's been a strange life: from Toronto to Detroit to England to Detroit to England to Ottawa to Montreal to Ottawa to Calgary to Ottawa. But a very long street connects them all—*Coronation Street*—and the awareness that excellence can take many forms, in many countries, and in many different media. That's the way it is when you are a survivor.

"You get up at 4 A.M for five years, and it's hard to think of something to say"

So he used "pull," which is never to be ignored in this business. CJOH station in Ottawa is 20 percent owned by Granada Television, which happily pushed for him to get the job of announcer. "I *wanted* to make my own career in Canada, but the old connection got me through the door!" He was there for about seven years. "I thought that I'd made a horrible mistake to come to Canada, but I decided subsequently that it was a *good* move, and I liked it." God bless foreign ownership of Canadian resources.

STEAMED LAKE TROUT

INGREDIENTS

1 gutted trout, whole
Coarse sea salt
Fresh ginger, chopped
Onion greens, finely chopped

INSTRUCTIONS

Take one whole gutted trout and score the outer flesh with 1/4-inch-deep cuts in a crisscross fashion 1 1/2 inches apart. Rub the fish inside and out with a mixture of 2 parts coarse sea salt, 1 part chopped fresh ginger, and 1 part finely chopped onion greens. Place fish on wire oven rack over boiling water in a wok. Cover until done, about 10 minutes, or until flesh comes away from the bone. Serve with head and tail, and steamed green beans.

WINE

A simple, classic dish demands a simple, classic wine—Sancerre or Pouilly Fumé from the Loire.

FRESH FRUIT SALAD

INGREDIENTS

Seedless green grapes
Bananas
Pears
McIntosh apples
Peaches
Walnut meats
Any other soft fruit in season
1 fresh lemon
Plain yogurt
Maple syrup
French brandy

INSTRUCTIONS

Dice, chop, or slice desired fruits. Squeeze the juice of fresh lemon over all. Mix in plain yogurt. Top with maple syrup and cheap French brandy to taste.

WINE

If you put enough cheap French brandy in, you won't need to drink anything else. Just sieve out the fruit, throw it away, and consume the liquid. Substitute Ontario brandy. It's cheaper.

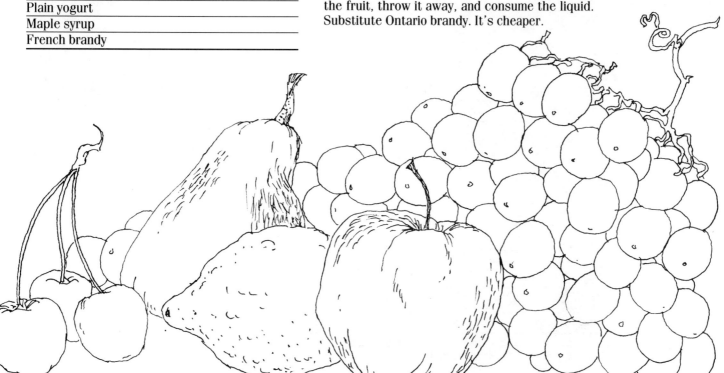

Vicki Gabereau

The radio host and ex-mayoralty candidate gets our vote for her Nearly Famous Burritos

*W*hen you tune in to *Variety Tonight* on weekday evenings and hear the lively, witty voice of Ms. Vicki Gabereau, do you realize that you are listening to a former Toronto mayoralty candidate?

You know now. Vicki Gabereau, in the guise of a clown named Rosie Sunrise, ran against David Crombie in the December 1974 election and came a strong fourth. True, the tiny perfect mayor (and, later, tiny perfect member of Parliament) received about 200,000 votes, while Gabereau/Sunrise was supported by 3,200 citizens. But the second- and third-place finishers *did* hurt a bit. One was a Communist (around 7,000) and the other was a member of the extreme-right-wing Western Guard (about 6,000 votes). But, as everyone who works for the CBC is aware, you cannot win them all.

Still, Vicki Gabereau has had a most interesting life, even when not running on such powerful platforms for mayor as "Let Crombie run the city in the day, and I'll run it at midnight, and be the night mayor." And the reverberations continue, even though "the children were mercifully too young to know." Recently, Gabereau's daughter Eve asked her mom, "You wouldn't be a clown and run for mayor again, *would* you?"

No, she wouldn't. What she *has* been doing since the fall of 1981—winning the treasured ACTRA Award for Best Host/Interviewer of an Entertainment Program in April, 1984—has been hosting *Variety Tonight*. And it looks as if the enjoyment—on both sides of the microphone— will continue.

Vicki Filion was born on May 31, 1946, in Vancouver, the same city from which she has been hosting her popular radio program since the summer of 1982. She quit school in Grade 12, got married at nineteen, and had two children from the union (which lasted for sixteen years): Morgan, now seventeen, and Eve, now fourteen.

Like most young mothers, Vicki Gabereau wanted to work, and work she did: as a waitress, as a hostess in a restaurant, in a geriatric nursing home. She even ran her own boutique business in Vancouver (in 1968), "selling it to the first sucker who responded to the advertisement, 'Dress Store for Sale, $5,000.'"

In 1970 she moved to Toronto with her husband and children, where her careers took a decidedly less traditional turn. In 1974 she "got into clowning," working with "Puck's Rent-a-Fool" and "Puck's Canadian Travelling Circus" for eighteen months. Then came that amazing run for mayor. And after that came a string of broadcasting and producing duties that would give a Crombie, a Communist, and a Fascist pause.

In 1975 Gabereau was invited to be a researcher for *Night Music*, a show on TV-Ontario. This was followed by a year-long shift on a radio station in Brampton, just outside Toronto. Then an actor called the executive producer of *Morningside* with the message that "there's some lunatic on that talk station in Brampton," which led to a researching job on that popular morning show ("now it would be called story producer").

More free-lance jobs followed: producing items for *Ideas, The Entertainers*, producing TV shows at TVO, culminating in her position as summer replacement for Don Harron in 1980, when she hosted *Morningside* for three months.

Yes, there was still more, including a season of doing the local CBC morning show in Edmonton (with Gayle Hulnick), in 1980–81, associate-producing *Thrill of a Lifetime* back in Toronto, and subsequently a call from Bruce Steele, the radio genius who created the kids' show *Anybody Home?* (on which Gabereau often worked), inviting her to take over *Variety Tonight*.

"My daughter asked, 'You wouldn't be a clown and run for mayor again, would you?'!"

Which brings us to today, 3,000 miles west of Toronto, but with the same show. Vicki Gabereau is again in her home town, living with a "man who works in the movie business" and her two children. "We entertain a lot," she says, "most often with one or two other couples. We play idiotic card games and shout at each other."

Gabereau confesses that her man "is a much better cook than I am." And she is distressed, as are many broadcasters, that they've never done any cooking items or food items on *Variety Tonight*, echoing Max Ferguson's dictum that "if you want to get letters, give a recipe!"

She is an "endless coffee drinker," and an "endless smoker," but neither has dampened her taste for good food. In Toronto, she loves to frequent the Hunan Palace and the Chung King Seafood Restaurant; in Vancouver, the Ferguson Point Tea Room in Stanley Park and Umberto's get her nod.

But, alas, alack-aday, Gabereau is like most of us: "I have slow metabolism and no exercise," and she finds herself fifteen pounds overweight. "If I ate chocolate, I'd weigh 200!" she moans. And with her entire family, with the exception of her mother, being "substantial," Vicki is following a tradition.

To those of you who might care to entice her during your next visit to CBC Vancouver, "I'd never refuse Nachos," Vicki Gabereau enthuses. And she probably found quite a few down in Los Angeles, when she went to help cover the 1984 Summer Olympics with Mark Lee, for CBC-Sports Radio.

But it's a fun existence, out in lovely Vancouver, entertaining hundreds of thousands of Canadians from coast to coast, five nights a week. And as long as she doesn't dress up as a clown again and run for mayor, the kids are happy, too. All that, and an ACTRA Award to boot. What more—with the exception of a little less rain and a better metabolism—could anyone want?

Vicki Gabereau and son
Morgan like to dine in
style.

NEARLY FAMOUS BURRITOS

INGREDIENTS

8 corn tortillas	8
1 onion, finely chopped	1
4 chicken breasts, cooked and diced	4
Lettuce, shredded	
2 tomatoes, peeled and diced	2
½ 14-oz. can ripe pitted olives, diced	½ 398-ml can
Hot Cha Cha Sauce (or salsa)	
Enchilada sauce	
Gouda cheese, shredded	
Green onions, sliced	
Sour cream	

INSTRUCTIONS

Place tortillas in oven-proof dish. To soften tortillas, drop 1 teaspoon water on them, cover with lid and bake at 300°F (150°C) for 10 minutes. Take out of oven. Prepare the following mixture: Put diced chicken into a bowl along with lettuce, tomatoes, onions, diced olives, and hot sauce to taste. Stir together. Fill tortillas generously with mixture. Fold like an envelope and turn seam side down. Cover with enchilada sauce and cheese. Place in oven at 350°F (180°C) for 10 minutes. Place burritos carefully on plates, at the same time calling the ambulance. Garnish with sour cream and green onions. Serve with guacamole and refried beans.

Serves 4-6

BEVERAGE

Forget about wine. Heroes will have tequila. Serve it at polar temperatures; wet rim of the glasses with lemon juice and encrust with sea salt. (Incidentally, how are things in Guacamole?)

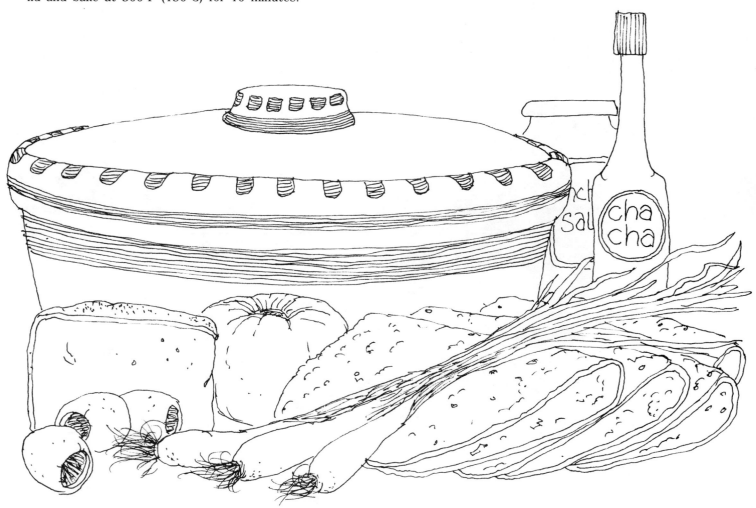

Clyde Gilmour

The host of Gilmour's Albums serves up a mean Pear Pie Pavarotti!

*C*lyde Gilmour is as straightforward as he is witty about his skills. He has studied singing "to an extent," and he can "read a score." But the only instrument he can play is "the phonograph, and I play it superbly. I think that it is the king of all the instruments, because it embraces them all."

His longtime stints prove how successful his playing has been: *The Happy Gang* lasted twenty-two years on CBC radio; *Farm Forum* was discontinued after twenty-six years. And on October 5, 1984, *Gilmour's Albums* (on which Mr. G. plays his instrument so very well) began its twenty-ninth year on the air, having begun in 1956.

For this, as for many things in all our lives, we can thank a set of parents. Born in Calgary (on June 8, 1912), raised in Edmonton, Lethbridge, and mainly Medicine Hat, Clyde Gilmour had a mother and father who were "keen about music, drama, and good, clean English and grammar." Most important, "they had a decent record collection. I grew up to feel that it was the natural thing to be listening to comedy by Harry Lauder, jazz, Caruso, and sentimental ballads."

It was an eclectic and catholic attitude toward music that has appealed to millions of listeners over the years. When I had a column in a major magazine, one question I put to famous people was about their favourite radio programs. "*Gilmour's Albums*," replied Margaret Trudeau. "*Gilmour's Albums*," answered Adrienne Clarkson. "*Gilmour's Albums*," we assume, would be spouted by many, many more.

Hopping about Western cities with a father who was chief clerk for the CPR would lead to similar drifting on his own. In 1936 Gilmour was working on the Edmonton Journal, having worked for the Medicine Hat *Journal*. Then, compliments of the Allies, he was off to Newfoundland, Londonderry, and London, then back to Canada and the Vancouver *Province*.

It was from there that we can trace the future critic. Gilmour did entertainment reporting at the *Province* and later at the *Sun*, and in the fall of 1947 he was called by CBC Vancouver to do movie reviews. He has been on the CBC radio network every week ever since, for thirty-seven years.

Older readers might recall, with pleasure, Gilmour's movie reviews for the major Sunday afternoon show, *Critically Speaking* (for which the great Nathan Cohen handled theatre), from 1949 to 1964.

The now-defunct Toronto *Telegram* offered him the job of movie critic in 1954, and there he laboured until the paper died in 1971. So he moved over to the Toronto *Star*, where he wrote movie reviews until the summer of 1980. "I've always had two jobs," he says.

His other big job since October 1956, of course, is *Gilmour's Albums*. "I knew several producers at CBC, and a number of them recommended that I do a show." He decided to do one that would play "my favourite music of all time—variety. At *no* time was it my concept to play all jazz or all classics." It began with a thirteen-week contract ("I expected that would be it"). They finally switched him to an annual contract, and you know how *that* turned out. (The initial weekly pay cheque was $50—ahh, the joys of free-lance.)

Behind many a successful long-running show is a spouse, of course. In Clyde Gilmour's case, it is his wife Barbara, née Donald, of Vancouver. Once head of sales of Hudson's Bay Book Department back in the 1950s, she has been "a tremendous help in research and filing. She answers 90 percent of the listeners' mail that comes in," which averages out to about 100 letters a month.

There have been two children of their happy union: Jane, thirty-one, is married and works as a personnel officer for the Ontario government;

"It was the natural thing to be listening to jazz and Caruso and sentimental ballads"

"I used to be able to scramble eggs. But unlike bicycling or swimming, one does forget!"

Paul, twenty-eight, is still single but more in his dad's line:—he sells classical records at a Sam the Record Man store.

Every day is a busman's holiday for the great phonograph player. The evening this interview took place, for instance, Gilmour played Alfred Brendel's new Beethoven Concerti during dinner (with the Chicago Symphony Orchestra, under James Levine). But he also likes "to play cheerful nightclub music when we eat, to talk over," such as Dick Hyman playing Scott Joplin rags.

The Gilmours do not entertain very much: "I keep too busy," and they don't go to large parties. As for cooking, Clyde Gilmour relies on Mrs. Gilmour. "I toast," he says, "and I'm a great can-opener. I *used* to be able to scramble eggs. But unlike bicycling or swimming, one does forget!"

So if you expected the same inspired serendipity in the Gilmour kitchen as you get on the Gilmour radio show, you can forget it. "I like to experiment with up to five different breakfast cereals in one bowl," he says. "Corn Flakes, Shredded Wheat, All-Bran, Rice Krispies, etc. I mix them all together, add a few blueberries and strawberries, and I can make a meal out of it." *Gourmet Magazine*, you have nothing to worry about.

If there is anything extraordinary about Gilmour's eating and drinking habits, it is his obsession with coffee—"up to twenty-five or thirty cups a day." For snacks he enjoys orange juice, raisins, nuts, apricots, apples, which he feels helps to explain why he's been "extremely free of colds and flu over the years."

But what Clyde Gilmour lacks in gourmet interests, he more than makes up for in his wonderful, all-embracing love of recordings, as captured, or at least hinted at, by his own record album, which covers ground from Judy Garland to Paul Brodie to Jerry Colonna to Pavarotti to Paul Robeson. For both the AM and stereo networks every week, for nearly three full decades now, the master of the phonograph continues to reign as king.

PEAR PIE PAVAROTTI

Not for calorie counters, but hard to resist. My wife Barbara names this after the famous tenor for three reasons: it has pears in it, Pav emits pear-shaped notes, and he himself is pear-shaped.

INGREDIENTS

4 oz. cream cheese	100 g
1/2 cup icing sugar	125 mL
2 tsp. vanilla	10 mL
3/4 cup whipping cream	175 mL
1 14-oz. can pear halves	1 398-mL can
1/2 cup grated chocolate	125 mL
1 9-inch baked pie shell	23 cm

INSTRUCTIONS

Beat cream cheese until soft. Add vanilla. Gradually add icing sugar, beating well. Whip cream and fold into cream cheese. Spread over baked pie shell. (If you prefer, a graham-cracker pie shell can be used instead.) Chill for 30 minutes. Drain pear halves and place them in a pattern over chilled pie. Sprinkle with grated chocolate and chill for 2 hours. Enjoy!
Serves 6

WINE

A sweet sparkling wine from the homeland of the great tenor himself, Asti Spumante. If the bubbles get up your nose, try the Italian dessert wine, Vin Santo (the grapes are left to dry until Christmas, then pressed and fermented).

RUMPPLE

My favourite alcoholic drink, and I claim it as my own, although I can't guarantee that nobody else has ever discovered the recipe. Note the double "p" in the name "Rumpple"; this indicates that it's a blend of rum and apple juice.

INGREDIENTS

2 oz. rum (light, amber, or dark)
Unsweetened apple juice
1/4 fresh lime
Ice cubes or crushed ice

INSTRUCTIONS

Put one good slug (2 ounces) of any good rum—light, amber, or dark, though I prefer the amber—into a large glass. If you chill the empty glass beforehand, all the better. Fill up with clear, *un*sweetened apple juice, but leave enough room for 4 or 5 ice cubes or a lot of crushed ice. Squeeze 1/4 fresh lime and drop the fruit into the glass. And sip *slowly*; Rumpple has food value that makes it easy on the system, but it can sneak up on you. It will mellow *any* disposition.
Serves 1

BEVERAGE

More of the same. Maritimers can substitute Newfoundland Screech with no ill effects. The rest of the country should stick to the designated rum.

Bill Good

Bill Good's pasta and pie recipes are very Good indeed

For Vancouver viewers and national sports fans, it must seem as if Bill Good has been going on forever. Well, he has, but in two generations. Bill Good, Sr., not only wrote for the Winnipeg *Tribune* but also did sports commentary for the CBC, covering everything from the Olympics to golf tours.

All this had a rather strong influence upon his namesake, Bill Good, Jr. Born in Winnipeg (on December 8, 1945), he moved out to British Columbia with his parents as a child, and soaked up what he observed his daddy doing: "I saw how much fun he was having, and decided to be in the business in one form or another."

And Bill Good *did* enter the biz, in one form or another. Straight from high school in 1965, he went into radio in Prince Rupert, opening CHTK up there. "I did *everything*, from covering the local council to doing the news run in the morning and the DJ run in the afternoon." (Small radio stations are usually the best training ground in the world.)

After a year there, Good went off to CFAX in Victoria, broadcasting in its news department (1966–67). In the Centennial Year he joined the CBC in Vancouver. He smiles: "I try not to remember how long ago it was."

He did the sign-on morning show for two years, and in 1969 came one of his biggest moves: when the Vancouver Canucks joined the National Hockey League, Bill Good joined CBC-TV sports. He announced *Hockey Night in Canada* with his city's team from 1969 to 1978, earning him well over a million fans, since that show has consistently been one of the most popular on television.

In 1978, Good switched over to news again, this time to anchor the 6-to-7 P.M. slot in Vancouver, called *News Centre*, along with Cecilia Walter. There has been no sports announcing since 1978, and he feels the loss. "I miss the people, and occasionally I miss covering a major event. But I find conventions interesting. And I've covered two provincial elections, two federal elections, and a lot of municipal ones." For anyone who is aware of the, shall we say volatile, political situation in British Columbia, it must almost be like describing a hockey game anyway.)

"I get a terrific challenge out of doing the live actuality broadcasts, whether conventions or elections," Good says. True, the Socreds and the NDP aren't in the same league as the 1972 and 1976 Olympics, or the amazing 1972 Russia–Canada hockey series, but they can be just as violent, passionate, and deeply involving, for broadcaster and audience alike.

Good is married and has three children: Brian, twelve, Shaela, eight, and three-year-old Derek, who is, in his father's delicate phrase, "hell on wheels!" His wife Georgena sells trade shows for

> *"I get a terrific challenge out of doing the live actuality broadcasts"*

The Goods (left to right): Bill, his wife Georgena, Derek, Brian, and Shaela. The poodle's name is Simon.

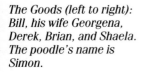

"I like all foods if they are well done..."

exhibitions, and the family enjoys one of the great locations in this country: their home in North Vancouver is just under the sky ride that goes up (and down) Grouse Mountain.

The Goods entertain every few weeks, one of the highlights being a gourmet group, consisting of four couples, which has met quarterly for five years now. Like most CBC personalities, Good prefers small dinner gatherings, except for Christmas Eve.

And foods? "I like all foods if they are well done—Italian, Greek, seafood, pasta dishes. As long as it's fattening, I love it."

And love it he does, although being six feet, five inches tall must help to hide the 200-plus pounds. (It can't hide the discomfort of the occasional guest, however. Bill Good laughs when he recalls a certain prominent politician who insisted upon sitting on two telephone books, because he feared looking shorter than the host of the TV news show. But how many of us would look *taller*?)

Other than height, Bill Good does not stand out terribly from the rest of us: he loves Scotch and

martinis, enjoys coffee, and gave up smoking last spring "when I just decided that it was time to quit."

Good, a downhill skier, goes off to Whistler with his family in the winter. And tennis and racquet ball provide summer exercise. Another hobby is his "constant restoring a 914 Porsche. It's one of the few sports cars that I fit comfortably in."

His favourite Vancouver restaurants include El Giardino of Umberto fame, as well as La Cantina and The Beach House—all of which move him toward the F-Plan, on which he now struggles. But as a chocolate freak "my whole life," he's searching for fibre that might be coated with either the milk or the bittersweet variety.

What it all comes down to is that Bill Good enjoys his life to the fullest. This only goes to show that going into your daddy's business can sometimes be very enjoyable and rewarding indeed.

PRIME TIME PASTA

INGREDIENTS

1/2 cup butter	125 mL
1 large clove garlic	1
1 medium onion, chopped	1
1 lb. asparagus, sliced into pieces	500 g
1/2 lb. mushrooms, sliced	250 g
1/2 lb. cauliflower, in flowers	250 g
1 medium zucchini, sliced	1
1 carrot, sliced	1
1 cup whipping cream	250 mL
1/2 cup chicken stock	125 mL
2 tbsp. fresh basil	30 mL
1 cup frozen peas	250 mL
2 oz. ham, chopped	50 g
5 green onions, chopped	5
1 lb. fettucine, cooked and drained	500 g
1 cup freshly grated Parmesan cheese	250 mL
1 lb. fresh shrimp, cooked	500 g

INSTRUCTIONS

Sauté butter, garlic, and onion in large deep skillet for 2 minutes. Add asparagus, mushrooms, cauliflower, zucchini, and carrot. Sauté for 2 minutes. Increase heat to high and add whipping cream, chicken stock, and basil. Boil to reduce mixture slightly. Stir in peas, ham, and green onions. Cook 1 minute. Add fettucine and Parmesan cheese. Toss it all together with cooked shrimp. Turn onto a platter and serve.
Serves 4 to 6

WINE

Tuck your serviette into your collar, pour yourself a beaker of Chianti Classico, and wade in during commercial breaks.

GRAND MARNIER CREAM PIE

INGREDIENTS

1/2 cup ground almonds	125 mL
3/4 cup vanilla wafer crumbs	175 mL
1/4 cup melted butter	50 mL
Grated rind of 1 orange	1
1 cup white sugar	250 mL
1/3 cup butter, softened	75 mL
8 oz. cream cheese, softened	250 g
2/3 cup Grand Marnier	150 mL
2 cups whipping cream	500 mL

INSTRUCTIONS

Combine almonds, vanilla wafer crumbs, and melted butter. Mix until nicely blended, and press into a 9-inch (23-cm) pie plate. Chill for a few minutes. Mix together orange rind, sugar, butter, and cream cheese. When well blended, beat in Grand Marnier. Set the mixture aside. Beat whipping cream until stiff, then fold it into the mixture and pour the combination into the pie crust. Set in the fridge for 3 or 4 hours. Great for after the show!
Serves 8

BEVERAGE

Have a control glass of Grand Marnier at your elbow to make sure the chef hasn't skimped. For the sybaritic, try the cream version of this liqueur.

Bill Guest

The star of Reach for the Top *has a chicken recipe nobody can top*

*H*ow many of us get to fulfill or live a childhood dream? The girl who attends the ballet and ends up a prima ballerina? The boy who collects baseball cards and ends up on one himself? Bill Guest, one of the best-loved radio and TV personalities of Winnipeg—and all of Canada, thanks to his hosting *Reach for the Top*—had just that experience.

As a child, he was "fascinated by radio." Born in the tiny town of Sioux Lookout, Ontario, on April 15, 1928, to a railroad man father, and raised in Redditt, about 128 miles to the west and "smaller still—under 400," he longed to be a radio announcer from his early teens. Guest recalls coming home from school around four o'clock each afternoon, sitting "with my ear to the radio, and listening to all the serials—*The Lone Ranger, Little Orphan Annie, The Air Adventures of Jimmie Allen, Talking Drums.*" He would read aloud from the paper, spouting off the ads.

When he was only seventeen years of age, a local station in Winnipeg (CKRC) invited him to audition. "You have a job," they told the eager kid. "Where do you want to work: Fort William or Yorkton, Saskatchewan?" Guest chose the former, CKPR, where he read the news, did DJ work, wrote continuity. After three years, moving up from $100 to $125 a month, he returned to CKRC in Winnipeg in 1948, where he was offered the towering sum of $175 a month. He replaced Jack Scott, who had done the *Superman* intros. "At the age of twenty, I was announcing the shows I loved as a kid!" Guest exclaims, still thrilled at the thought, over thirty-five years later.

Not that Bill Guest *had* to end up in broadcasting. He himself admits that if he hadn't clicked in that field, he "would have chosen railroads." Sioux and Redditt were on the CNR main line, and the latter was a divisional point. "Steam engines

were checked over in our town, and they'd put water in the boilers. A roundhouse was there. I smelled steam throughout my childhood."

From 1948 to 1958 he stayed with that small station in Winnipeg, "getting a good basic education," covering such highlights as the annual Santa Claus parade. He married in 1954, had a son, Bill Jr., in 1958 (who recently received an MBA from the University of Manitoba), and began doing TV, handling royal tours, traffic mobiles, and kids' talent shows.

But his "greatest coup," he admits, was taking over as quizmaster of *Reach for the Top* from Warren Davis, in 1963, when the latter went to Toronto. "The program took me to play-offs across the country, and many brilliant kids went through it." (The fondest memory is from the 1967 game, broadcast from Expo in Montreal,

"At the age of twenty, I was announcing the shows I loved as a kid!"

weather, and it starred himself and a rooster, "which was *supposed* to go to sleep during the total eclipse, but did not!"

Other shows included TV's *Tandem*, on which Guest and a co-host toured summer attractions around Winnipeg on a bicycle built for two. But most important, without doubt, is the fact that Winnipeg introduced the "info radio" concept to CBC back in 1969-70, and Guest has been involved in morning broadcasts "off and on" since that date. The hours are rough—"you've got to get up pretty early for a show that runs 6-to-9 A.M. every weekday."

Bill Guest also has plenty of outside interests. He is keenly interested in photography and has "probably the only Land Rover in the world that is air-conditioned" to let him drive through swamps and bush. He also does a lot of fishing, hooking up a seventeen-foot trailer and heading off "to any lake that appeals to me."

Guest and his wife do not entertain very often —"In this business, we want time for ourselves when we're away from it." However, he fancies himself a "good soup-cooker. You have to be careless and throw in lots of things that others abhor." He loves Chinese and Italian cuisines, and admits that, while he is "not gross," he does weigh over 200, "which is far too heavy."

He gave up smoking some twenty years ago, and the reason why is typical of the business. "Even *before* it became fashionable to quit, I did," he insists, having smoked two packs a day when he was on radio. But "the coming of TV stopped me smoking. I couldn't cut off the mike to cough on TV as I could do on radio."

Bill Guest has come a long way from Sioux Lookout and Redditt, spiritually if not geographically. Listening to jazz records, doing a little cartooning, listening to short-wave broadcasts from the BBC, travelling with his wife on tours to Switzerland and France—it's an exciting life.

And, as far as many Canadians are concerned, the railway's loss was broadcasting's gain. Radio waves could always travel farther and faster than trains anyway.

"The coming of TV stopped me smoking. I couldn't cut off the mike to cough on TV as I could on radio."

when Britain's top team played the best of Canada's *Reach* grads. One of the questions was "Who was England's queen at the end of the nineteenth century?" to which one student yelled "Oscar Wilde." The kid was serious, and not all that wrong either.)

There have been other broadcasting highlights as well. For instance, it was Bill Guest who did a full network broadcast of the total eclipse of the sun, in 1979. "We had an audience bigger than the Walt Disney show had," recalls Guest, because the show came on at 11 A.M., and was picked up in schools right across Canada. He did it from the roof of the CBC building, in subzero

THE WEST'S BEST CHICKEN BREAST

INGREDIENTS

4 oz. chicken breast	100 g
1/4 cup mango chutney	50 mL
1/2 cup brown sauce (or gravy)	125 mL
4 oz. puff pastry	100 g
1 slice toast	1
1 egg, beaten (for egg wash)	1
Salt and pepper, to taste	
Vegetable oil	

INSTRUCTIONS

Cut chicken breast into slices and season with salt and pepper. Sauté chicken slices in vegetable oil. Add brown sauce and mango chutney, and cook for about 2 minutes, until sauce is reduced. Roll puff pastry until it is 8 inches (20 cm) in diameter and about 1/2 inch (1.25 cm) thick. Place toast in the middle of the pastry, then place chicken on top of toast. Wrap pastry, tucking in the edges. Brush beaten egg wash on surface of pastry. Bake at 400°F (200°C) for about 15 minutes, until golden brown.
Serves 1

WINE

The mango chutney complicates the wine choice. Liebfraumilch would do, but a German Riesling Spätlese would be better.

EGGS ASSINIBOINE

The taste of these eggs will have you repeating the ritual, at least one day a week, for the rest of your days!

INGREDIENTS

1 lb. spinach	500 g
8 slices finest back bacon	8
4 farm fresh eggs	4
Hollandaise sauce:	
2 egg yolks	2
1/2 cup unsalted butter	125 mL
2 teaspoons lemon juice	10-mL
Dash of cayenne pepper	a dash
2 English muffins	
Paprika	
Salt and pepper	
Unsalted butter	

INSTRUCTIONS

Rinse the spinach in cold water. Don't dry it, but boil it in the water gathered during the rinse for about 5 minutes (or until it's limp). Start frying the bacon and toasting the muffins lightly. *To prepare Hollandaise sauce:* Place the 2 egg yolks in the top of a double boiler over simmering water. Begin whisking immediately, adding the butter gradually (4 or 5 pieces evenly chopped). Keep stirring until the sauce is thick. Then add fresh lemon juice and a touch of cayenne pepper. Poach the 4 eggs for 4 minutes. *To assemble:* Use half a muffin as the base for each serving. Butter each piece lightly, then add 2 slices of bacon, followed by a suitable amount of well-drained spinach. Add the egg and top with a generous coating of sauce. Salt and pepper to taste. Add a dash of paprika for colour. Note: If the Hollandaise sauce should separate during the mixing, try adding a few drops of cold water while you're whisking. It should come back together!
Serves 4

WINE

A dry but full sparkling wine (Champagne if you're celebrating, Spanish cava for everyday triumphs). Red Bordeaux or white Graves would also fill the Bill.

Bob Homme

The Friendly Giant does wonderful things with a rabbit

Bob Homme, who has been asking Canadian children to look up—"waaaaay up"—since the fall of 1958 (and American children since four years before *that*), has a number of delightful food memories, which befits a very friendly giant.

"Rusty the Rooster is the baker on the show," he says. "I make a teeny sourdough bread and arrange with him to hold it up to Jerome (the Giraffe). Jerome says 'thank you,' but you can see that he's disappointed because it's so small. Then Rusty begins to pull out an *endless* French bread from his bag for Jerome."

A sweet gag, and a warm one—just like *The Friendly Giant* show, and just like Bob Homme (rhymes with Mummy). As two generations of parents and children know, this ain't *Sesame Street*, filled with thirty-second cartoons and thirty-second *Laugh-In*-type sketches. As Homme puts it, "We're trying to stretch the attention span of children."

Homme was born on March 8, 1919, in Stoughton, Wisconsin, and educated at the university in Madison, in the field of labour problems, believe it or not. But while attending school, he became interested in the local radio station and "spent a lot of time there." He decided to remain in that field—and later TV—and never did return to the field of labour.

He worked as a music programmer, then got into radio for children, doing poetry, songs, and stories. When TV began in around 1953, "I searched for an idea to convert my radio show into a television one. Most of the ones on the air were clowns. You know, 'Hey, Kids!!'"

The "Giant" concept came to him eventually, and the first view of that very friendly, tall man was on Madison, Wisconsin, television, back in May, 1954, over three decades ago. A nice bit of trivia that probably few knew before now, even though they may have wondered: "The show signed on at 6:45 P.M., so it was a going-to-bed program for toddlers; the last thing they would watch at night. That's why the moon comes up and the cow jumps over the moon at the show's close. We kept that when it went to the morning." Now you know.

The story of how Bob Homme came up to our Home and Frozen Land is also rather touching, and a nice nod to our long-suffering servants at the CBC. After doing *The Friendly Giant* on a daily basis for WHA Radio in Madison and being bicycled to nearly a dozen stations across the United States, including Boston, New York, St. Louis, Chicago, and L.A., he noticed something fascinating at various conferences: "I'd meet representatives of other TV networks. There'd be one guy from ABC, another from NBC, but there would be

Bob and Esther Homme outside their home near Cobourg, Ontario.

When TV began, "I searched for an idea to convert my radio show into a television one"

"I liked Toronto so much, I asked if I could stay for thirteen weeks. That was twenty-six years ago!"

a half-a-dozen writers and producers from the CBC. Here was a whole *department* for children!"

So in the spring of 1958, when Homme was invited to do a live children's show on Sunday afternoon's *Junior Magazine*, he came to Canada with a wife, all four children (the youngest was only ten days old), his complete props, and a canoe on the top of his station wagon. Another nice story here: when he brought his castle up, it had plastic vines all over it. Canada Customs thought he had "some exotic kind of plant" with him, and held him up a while.

"I liked Toronto so much, I asked if I could stay for thirteen weeks." He originally had a year's leave of absence from the Madison TV station, and he kept renewing. But as *The Friendly Giant* went from two to three times a week and to daily by the third year, he "parlayed the thirteen weeks into twenty-six years!"

Back in the States, you should know, there was only Rusty the Rooster. "I couldn't get a good giraffe," Homme says; "then I met Rod Coneybeare, and he took to Jerome (the Giraffe) immediately. It transforms you to put a big puppet on your hand!" Homme's partner in entertainment does both voices and "has no trouble. If he goofs a line, the other voice can correct him."

There was a daily radio show on CBC, as some of you might remember, on Saturdays, called *Mr. Homme's House*, and *Just for Fun*, which evolved into *The Kid's Show*. But it's the Giant who has carried the giant-sized load of Bob Homme's time, over the past thirty years.

Nowadays, Bob Homme and wife Esther entertain less than they used to, because they live about seventy-five miles east of Toronto, near Cobourg. When time permits, he swims and hikes to keep himself in fairly good shape. With the kids grown up and out of the house now, they both cook, with his wife "doing the lion's share. She's better at it." Still, our Giant does a lot of barbecuing and reads *Gourmet Magazine* and other food articles regularly. He likes good coffee and good wine, and he enjoys good restaurants, such as Fenton's, from whom he stole their lapin pie recipe. When he decided to try making that rabbit dish, "my wife thought it was foolish, but I thought it would be great." In classic TV sit-com fashion, the wife was correct. "As the guests arrived, all the dough sank down to the bottom! It was kind of a fiasco. But it was good, too—more like a stew with an interesting dumpling on the bottom!"

When I asked him to think back to his most favourite food gag of all, it didn't take him too long to come up with this one: "We did a popcorn thing a few times on the show. Rusty wants to make popcorn, and Jerome keeps saying 'More! More! Just a shade more!' Finally there is too much. But Rusty takes it into his book bag, and you hear Rusty shaking it on a stove in the bag. You hear corn popping, and Rusty screaming, 'I can't hold the top down! It's too much!'"

At this point special effects comes in, with a snow machine full of popcorn exploding everywhere across the screen, with Jerome Giraffe trying to catch the kernels. "It's worked each time!" says Bob Homme, the Friendly Giant.

One could say the same about his lovely perenniel show.

RABBIT AND WILD RICE CASSEROLE

INGREDIENTS

1 rabbit, including bones	1
1 cup wild rice	250 mL

To prepare marinade:

3 cups buttermilk	750 mL
1 bay leaf	1
6 peppercorns	6
3 sprigs fresh thyme or ¼ teaspoon dried thyme	1 mL
1 clove garlic, peeled and halved	1
1 medium onion, sliced	1

To cook the bones:

1 tbsp. oil	15 mL
1 tbsp. butter	15 mL
½ cup dry white wine	125 mL
1 medium onion	1
1 clove garlic	1
salt and pepper	

To sauté rabbit:

2 tbsp. oil	30 mL
1 tbsp. butter	15 mL
½ cup dry white wine	125 mL

To assemble casserole:

3 tbsp. butter	45 mL
2 cups mushrooms	500 mL
½ cup chopped onion	125 mL
½ cup chopped celery	125 mL
1 10-oz. can celery soup	1 284-mL can
1 cup broth (reserved from meat and bones)	250 mL
1 tsp. salt	5 mL
½ cup hazelnuts, chopped	125 mL

INSTRUCTIONS

Cut meat from rabbit into pieces as large as possible. Don't be afraid to leave a bit on the bones; nothing will be wasted. Cut the meat into bits about the size of large button mushrooms. *To prepare marinade*: Combine buttermilk, bay leaf, peppercorns, thyme, garlic, and onion. Place rabbit in bowl with marinade, cover, and leave in refrigerator overnight. *To cook the bones*: Sauté bones in skillet with oil and butter until brown. Add white wine (Vermouth is also good), onion, garlic, salt, and pepper. Simmer until meat on bones is tender. Remove meat and bones from skillet. Reserve the broth with scrapings from the bottom of the skillet. Pick the bones for lunch. Enjoy! *To prepare wild rice*: Put rice in top of double boiler and cover with boiling water. Cook, covered, over simmering water for 1 hour or until rice is tender. Stir occasionally, adding water if needed. (If you have your own favourite way of preparing wild rice, use it.) *To sauté the rabbit*: Remove rabbit from marinade. Place on a cookie sheet and pat dry with a paper towel. Discard marinade. Heat 2 tablespoons (30 mL) of oil and 1 tablespoon (15 mL) of butter in skillet and brown meat, a few pieces at a time, removing to a bowl when browned. When all the meat is done, drain excess fat from skillet. Return meat to skillet, add dry white wine and bring to a boil, scraping up browned bits in pan. Sprinkle with salt and pepper. Cover pan and simmer until meat is tender, approximately 1 hour. Remove cover for the last 15 minutes. Reserve broth with scrapings from skillet. Combine with previously reserved broth, and add water to equal 1 cup (250 mL), if necessary. *To assemble the casserole*: Sauté onions, mushrooms, and celery in butter. Combine celery soup and broth in saucepan. Heat and stir until smooth. Add sautéed vegetables, salt, half the nuts, and rabbit pieces. Mix with wild rice and place in buttered casserole. Sprinkle remaining nuts on top. Cover and bake 1 hour at 350°F (180°C).

Serves 6

WINE

Red wines from the lesser French regions like Corbières, Côtes de Duras, or Cabernet Franc from the Loire. In honour of the Friendly Giant, serve in tall glasses from magnums.

Gail Hulnick

The host of Vancouver's Early Edition *breakfasts on bagels and coffee*

*T*his is a tale of the luck of the Irish. And the luck of the Ukrainian, too, since Gail Hulnick is half of each. "My father is Ukrainian, my mother is Irish," she says, "so I get the partying from my dad's side, and the temper from my mom's."

Gail Hulnick was born in Edmonton, on September 25, 1954, and she moved around a lot: her father was and is an accountant for MacMillan Bloedel, the giant lumber firm, so she grew up in Edmonton, Winnipeg, and Toronto, spending about an equal period in each.

Even her college career was peripatetic: she studied at the University of Toronto and the University of Alberta in Edmonton, and received a journalism degree at Western, in London, Ontario. Then she earned an MBA at the University of Alberta.

Hulnick had "always been interested in journalism," and although the initial interest was print, at Western, the teachers made the students "go through all three media. I enjoyed the added dimension of voice and visuals."

The first job was with CBC-TV in Windsor, Ontario, as part of the trainee program that the CBC runs, taking about a dozen students from Ryerson, Western, and Carleton and putting them to work for four months. "I did a whole range of things, from 'kindergarten kids take train trip' to covering the 1977 provincial election." No, it "wasn't too scary," since she could do lots of takes and "edit out the embarrassing parts."

Then, like hundreds of thousands of other Canadians in the late '70s, Hulnick wanted to go west, although in *her* case, it was to "go back." All the stories in the papers about the energy boom affected her, too. So when she got an offer from the CTV affiliate in Edmonton to cover the Alberta legislature for CFRN (competition of the CBC), she moved back to her birthplace.

By 1979 she was back at the CBC. She heard of an opening on an afternoon radio show, and she "wanted to talk with people for *six* minutes instead of one and a half." A fitting put-down of the tendency of television to serve everything in bite-sized portions.

In 1981, Hulnick had a perfectly good job, as co-host of *Edmonton AM* (along with good friend Vicki Gabereau, now at *Variety Tonight*). "Then I wanted to get married," she says. Her fiancé was a lawyer out in Vancouver and she had to make that dangerous choice which so many spouses—usually women, alas—have to make: Do I give up my career for *him*?

"The usual pattern is to go from radio to TV. I did it backwards!"

She did. Gail Hulnick quit her radio job in Edmonton and moved out to Vancouver without a job. "It was purely a matter of luck," she says. "The guy who hosted the morning show in Vancouver quit, by chance, just two weeks after I moved out here!" And so, since September 1981, she has been host of the *Early Edition* in Vancouver. "The usual pattern is to go from radio to TV," she notes, "I did it backward." And she loves it. "Radio is so intimate!" she exclaims. "Something happens across town, and you just pick up a phone."

Not that she loves every aspect of it. "I get up Monday through Friday at 4:30 A.M., and I *hate* it!" She needs that morning coffee: "I couldn't get started without it." But she sleeps in the afternoons so that she can have "a normal sort of evening until 11:00 P.M. Otherwise, I couldn't

have an normal life." Which she does, enjoying interviewing such personalities as Hugh MacLennan, the famous Canadian author—"one of the most charming men I've ever met. The six-minute interview turned into twenty. I didn't want to let him out of the studio." Of course, there have been "a few people who freeze up and give me two-word answers!"

Not surprisingly, with her busy life, Gail Hulnick splits the cooking with her lawyer-husband, Barry Galbraith: "We each have our specialties; he's good at brunches, I'm good at desserts."

She recalls one of the dangers of radio: giving a recipe too rapidly. One Christmas after the show a listener called in with a recipe for home-made Irish cream "cheaper than bottled!" Hulnick put the recipe in her pocket as "filler material." Then, when she had two minutes to spare a few days later, she slid it in, "reading it off too quickly."

You can guess what happened. "For weeks afterward, we had people phoning the studio saying, 'She read it too fast!' It was *really* popular." Even six months later, Hulnick was getting letters that read: Do you still have that Irish cream recipe around?"

It's a good life out in Vancouver: Hulnick and spouse love to go to the Cannery restaurant, with its fresh fish and "the great view of the boats coming into the harbour." Another favourite is Hy's Mansion, an old family home in Vancouver's West End, with "mahogany everywhere, a big fireplace, and huge leather chairs to sit in for drinks before dinner." They also enjoy dining at The William Tell Restaurant.

At home, they snack on popcorn while watching movies on their VCR; or on Sunday they take a five-minute walk over to the Granville market for bagels, coffee, and newspapers. Photography is a year-round hobby, as well as reading, seeing plays, and skiing in winter. "Whistler is so close," she beams. "It's as if you've been dropped into Switzerland! It's a dream world." Talk about lucky Irish-Ukrainians.

BROCCOLI CASSEROLE

This is great as a meal all by itself or as a vegetable side dish at dinner after you've had a really active day, skiing for instance.

INGREDIENTS

1 large onion, chopped	1
1/4 cup butter	50 mL
4 cups fresh broccoli, chopped to bite size	1 L
1 cup fresh mushrooms, sliced	250 mL
1/2 cup almonds, chopped	125 mL
1 cup long grain rice	250 mL
1 10-oz. can cream of mushroom soup	1 284-mL can
1 cup sharp cheddar cheese, grated	250 mL
1/2 cup breadcrumbs, buttered	125 mL

INSTRUCTIONS

Sauté onion in butter. Spoon into large casserole dish. Boil broccoli in water until crunchy. Drain and add to casserole. Add mushrooms and almonds (set some almonds aside for topping). Cook rice according to package directions and add to casserole.

In a separate bowl, blend mushroom soup and cheese. Add to the casserole. Top with reserved almonds and buttered breadcrumbs and bake at 350°F (180°C) for 35–45 minutes.
Serves 10 for 1 meal—or 1 for a week

WINE

A light red wine like Beaujolais or rosé.

BAKED STUFFED FISH

Fish is one of my favourite things to serve. In a coastal city you can always have it fresh and it's so simple to prepare.

INGREDIENTS

2–3 lbs. whole fish	1–1.5 Kg
1 1/4–1 1/2 cups stuffing	300–375 mL
1/4 cup butter, melted	50 mL
2 tbsp. lemon juice	30 mL
2 tbsp. fresh parsley, finely chopped	30 mL
1/2 tsp. salt	2 mL
1/8 tsp. pepper	a pinch

Stuffing:

2 cups soft breadcrumbs	500 mL
1/4 cup butter, melted	50 mL
2 tsp. lemon juice	10 mL
1/4 cup chopped walnuts	50 mL
1/4 tsp. nutmeg	1 mL
Salt and pepper to taste	

INSTRUCTIONS

For the stuffing, mix together butter and breadcrumbs. Add other ingredients and mix thoroughly. Clean, scale, and stuff fish loosely. Truss with string and place in greased pan. Mix melted butter, lemon juice, parsley, and seasonings and pour over the fish. (For a change, you could substitute dry white wine.) Bake at 450°F (220°C) for 10 minutes per inch (2.5 cm) of thickness of the stuffed fish at the thickest part.
Serves 4 to 6

WINE

Dry white wine. Depending on the fish: mild-flavoured—crisp Riesling; oily, full-flavoured—dry white Burgundy or Chardonnay or even rosé.

Tommy Hunter

The King of the Airwaves admits that he is not the Prince of the Kitchen

*I*t may not be the epitome of country cuisine, but Tommy Hunter is "partial to peanut butter." The reason for his affection will be familiar to anyone who has worked long and hard years to achieve success: "When I first came to Toronto, I was struggling," says the six-foot-four star of the hugely popular CBC-TV show that bears his name. "There were a lot of lean days, and a lot of travelling and learning. I played every bar and honkytonk across Canada. I'd work one day, then be off six months. A loaf of bread and peanut butter went a long way to fill your belly."

So much for overnight success. And so much for *haute cuisine*, for that matter. But maybe it's that sense of paying your dues that gives both Hunter's show and his singing the power they possess.

Born on March 20, 1937, in the not-so-country city of London, Ontario, he was an only child, with no phone, no car, but with a father over at the CN Railway whose work with the steam engines made Tommy Hunter, to this day, "a railway nut." But he is a singer, not a train man, and it was his first exposure to country music that changed his life forever. A Grand Ole Opry show came to the London arena, and from the moment he saw and heard Roy Acuff and his Smoky Mountain Boys and Girls, he was hooked. By the time he was eleven, he was "so into guitar I knew it was my life."

In 1955, soon after CBC-TV first went on the air, the young Tommy Hunter was playing guitar in a band, and singing solo once a week, when he was invited to be a summer replacement for *Holiday Ranch*. The show was called *Country Hoedown*, it survived nine long years, and it starred such other people as fiddler King Ganam, singers Tommy Common, Lorraine Foreman, and the Hames Sisters, and an emcee by the name of Gordie Tapp.

If you are over forty, you probably remember it; one third of the three million television sets in this country were tuned to that show every Friday night. And then, just short of its tenth birthday it evolved into *The Tommy Hunter Show*, thirty minutes long for a few years, and then sixty minutes after that.

Fall 1984 marked the twentieth year of the *TH Show*, with no end in sight. Not that the show is the be-all and end-all of Tommy Hunter's life; he has been happily married to his wife Shirley since before he got his own program, and he bursts with pride over his three sons: Jeff, twenty-one, who sells real estate; Greg, nineteen, a professional airline pilot, and Mark, still in high school.

But if Tommy Hunter is King of the Airwaves—his two-million-plus ratings place him right up there with the handful of CBC-TVs most popular shows—he isn't even Prince of the Kitchen. "My wife is *such* a good cook," he laughs, "that I finally backed out of that room and let her take over." Not that Hunter is incompetent. "I love to use my chafing dishes," he explains, and delights in entertaining a few close friends ("I cherish their conversation dearly") with the chafing dish as "the main entertainment focal point."

As he puts it, "We sit down, have a leisurely salad, prepare everything at the table, and carry on the conversation without all the continuous up-and-down."

Being the star of a variety show is echoed in Hunter's tastes in food. "I like variety. I love to catch and cook my own fish when we're down in Florida." (The Hunters go to their condo just north of West Palm Beach after Christmas each year, returning around the first of June.) "I also like to go to my favourite seafood places and eat there." So what's the variety? "I love nothing

By the time he was eleven, he was "so into guitar I knew it was my life"

Tommy and his wife Shirley having coffee off the set of The Tommy Hunter Show.

"I love nothing more than a good stew on a blustery, snowy evening"

more than a good stew on a blustery, snowy evening—but after two nights of that, I'm ready for something else."

Hunter doesn't drink at all—"no wine, beer, anything. I'll drink Perrier with a twist of lime." It's ironic because, as every country fan knows, "ninety percent of all country songs are about drinking. The other ten percent are about gambling, dying, and chasing women."

Not that nothing liquid goes down those famous vocal cords. "I drink far too much coffee," he confesses. "I like chickory and am always looking for various blends, whether New Orleans or Jamaican-type." And, yes, he *does* smoke, but "I hope to quit soon."

For a man of music, he dislikes hearing it in restaurants: "I don't like having to holler over a piano player. I feel guilty eating and not paying attention to the piano player!" However, as he says, "We don't eat out all that much." The family

likes suburban restaurants not far from their new home in Caledon Hills—a real country setting—but they really don't have much time to go out often. "We're gone six months a year and when I'm here in Toronto, I'm busy rehearsing and taping TV shows all the time."

A sense of responsibility runs through Hunter's life: to family, and to his career. "I have to *learn* everything before I go *anywhere*," he admits. "I can't leave my house until I've memorized all the songs and talk for each show. I just sit at home, and relax, and keep going over it."

So for those millions of you who watch Tommy Hunter each week and think that it looks so easy, you're wrong. The man who has never lost his taste for peanut butter has never lost his taste for hard work either.

SPECIAL STEAK

INGREDIENTS

2 filet steaks	2
1/4 cup Scotch	50 mL
1/4 cup sweet red pimentos, chopped	50 mL
1 medium onion, chopped	1
1 tbsp. parsley flakes	15 mL
Black pepper, to taste	
3/4 cup table cream	175 mL
1/2 cup whipping cream	125 mL
1/4 cup sherry	50 mL

INSTRUCTIONS

In a chafing dish, grill steaks until medium rare. Pour in Scotch, then ignite steaks. When flame has died down, transfer steaks to a separate dish. In chafing dish, prepare sauce as follows. Combine pimentos, onion, parsley, and black pepper. Mix table and whipping cream together with sherry; combine with the dry ingredients and cook sauce until onions are soft. Return steaks to chafing dish and heat through.

Serves 2

WINE

Châteauneuf-du-Pape or Baco Noir. For total abstainers like Tommy, accompany the dish with Concord grape juice or *As It Happens*.

Jay Ingram

One quirk of Quirks and Quarks host is his love of pasta

*I*t is hard to imagine Jay Ingram, the ACTRA Award-winning host of CBC-radio's extremely popular science show, *Quirks and Quarks*, ever passing up a chance to study something different and exciting. But, he confesses, he actually did in his youth. His father worked for Hudson's Bay for his entire career, running northern stores up in the Arctic. "Stupidly, I never went up with him," Ingram says today; "it never seemed to be offered."

But mark that down to the foolishness of youth. There are few things that Ingram has *not* experienced since then. Born in Winnipeg on March 20, 1945, he grew up in that prairie city until he was in Grade 11, when his family moved to Edmonton. He went to the University of Alberta, earning a B.Sc. in microbiology, fulfilling an interest extending back to his pre-teens. Ingram owned a microscope by Grade 6, and "was a reasonably accomplished bird watcher by then." Now the owner of a tiny yard in the Cabbagetown section of Toronto, he is currently "making the transition to watching insects."

After graduating from U. of A. in the Centennial Year, he took a year off to explore Europe, travelling in a VW van, and then came back to do graduate work in microbiology at the University of Toronto. After that, Ingram moved on to take a doctorate in embryology at McMaster University in nearby Hamilton. And then came the kind of crisis that often hits eternal students when they realize that they just might be boxing themselves into a field where they might not be happy. "I realized that I didn't *really* want to specialize and become a researcher."

So in 1972 Ingram took a job teaching chemistry and biology at Ryerson Polytechnical Institute, where, to be succinct, "I enjoyed it." That lasted about a year and a half, at which point his contract expired. But—the first inkling of his future success as a radio-show host—he *did*

teach a biology course on CJRT radio, the popular and influential education/volunteer/noncommercial station of Ryerson, in 1975–76.

Then began free-lance work in 1976, and his fame started to spread: *Morningside, The Bob McLean Show*, articles on science for the *Globe and Mail*. (He was married for seven years during this period.) Finally, in 1979, he was (wisely) invited to join *Quirks and Quarks* as its host, replacing David Suzuki. This forced him to give up his other CBC assignments—but not give up everything. His favourite *other* job is his role as

"I realized that I didn't really want to specialize and become a researcher"

And then there is food. Ingram and Cynthia "entertain often," usually inviting small numbers of people at a time and dividing the cooking duties evenly. "We both love pasta," he says. And he loves ham, but "I never run into anyone who likes it," he claims. And Jay Ingram is the kind of man who can drink "California and Italian wines and can tell the difference." (Whether he can do that scientifically or not is unknown).

With all that knowledge of science which he has, and which he shares so generously with all of us each week, it's not surprising that he doesn't smoke. But he *does* love coffee—"with a passion." And he insists that India Gardens, a Winnipeg restaurant, "is the best I've ever eaten in, and that includes Liverpool and London."

Of course, in a science show, Ingram has occasionally spoken on matters of food. Dare I mention the one item that fascinated our host the most? It was a piece on cannibalism, some time ago. "The argument was whether or not it was done by the Aztecs for ecological reasons rather than as ritual. It was due to a lack of food, so the Aztecs began to use other cultures as stockyards. You see, I like when you take an existing set of data and give a new twist to it."

Not the stuff of a cookbook, perhaps, but definitely an insight into why Jay Ingram is such a marvelous scientist who carries us with him into the excitement of his subjects.

Oh yes, it all ends up neatly sooner or later: Jay Ingram finally *did* get up to the North. He spoke to a group up in the Yukon, recently, on "Keeping Warm." But you only have to flick on your radio each Saturday, to hear Jay Ingram speaking on *anything* scientific. And nowadays, that means almost *everything*.

"I like when you take an existing set of data and give a new twist to it"

contributing editor to *Owl* Magazine—"I'm constantly working for them"—the superb science periodical for children ages eight and over, published by the Young Naturalist Foundation in Toronto (which also puts out *Chickadee* for younger folk). Recently Ingram submitted about 250 questions to the new Junior Trivial Pursuit, but it will probably never be his major claim to fame. Or wealth.

But Ingram is not in it for the money. There are more important things in the world, such as his lady, Cynthia Dann-Beardsley, with whom he lives. (She does "a lot of programming for CJRT," the same Ryerson radio station where Ingram got his broadcasting start.) And his love of golf, touch football, archeology, and (believe it or not) video games.

Poulet Aux Deux Moutardes

INGREDIENTS

3-lb. chicken, cut into 8 portions	1.5 Kg
2 tbsp. flour	30 mL
Salt	
Freshly ground pepper	
2 tbsp. olive oil	30 mL
2 tbsp. butter	30 mL
4 shallots, chopped	4
Bouquet garni	
1 cup chicken stock	250 mL
1/4 cup dry Vermouth	50 mL
1 tbsp. Dijon mustard	15 mL
1 tsp. dry English mustard (or more, to taste)	5 mL
1/2 cup whipping cream	125 mL

INSTRUCTIONS

Dredge chicken pieces in flour. Add salt and pepper and sauté in oil and butter in a large skillet until golden. Add chopped shallots and bouquet garni. Moisten with stock and Vermouth. Cook gently, covered, until tender. Place chicken on a warm serving platter. Add both mustards to the cream and mix thoroughly with a wire wisk. Add chicken stock-Vermouth sauce. Correct seasoning to taste. Add chicken. Heat thoroughly and serve.

Serves 4

WINE

A strongly flavoured dish calling for substantial red wines like Californian Zinfandel, Rhone reds, or Corvo from Sicily.

Mustard Baked Eggs

INGREDIENTS

1/4 lb. old cheddar, freshly grated	125 g
4 eggs	4
6 tbsp. table cream	75 mL
1 tsp. dry mustard (or more, to taste)	5 mL
Dash of cayenne pepper	a dash
1/2 tsp. salt	2 mL
1 tbsp. butter	15 mL

INSTRUCTIONS

Preheat oven to 350°F (180°C). Sprinkle grated cheese over the bottom of a buttered 9-inch (23-cm) square pan or pie plate. Break the eggs over the cheese, but be careful not to break the yolks. Combine cream, mustard, cayenne pepper, and salt. Pour over eggs. Dot with butter. Bake for 15 to 20 minutes, or until eggs are set. Do not overbake! The eggs should remain creamy inside.

Serves 4

WINE

Jay has a thing about mustard. Again, bold reds are required. Try a Garrafeira from Portugal.

Christine Johnson

This TV co-host says her place is in the Market Place

*I*f there is anyone who captures Alexander Pope's famous line about how "the twig is bent, the tree's inclined," it is Christine Johnson, the co-host of *Market Place* since the fall of 1983. First of all, "as the oldest of twelve children, I had lots of experience raising children!" And ditto for why she "got into consumerism. You learn to be thrifty when you have a large family!"

Of course, there is a lot more to consumerism than saving money; it has to do with health, concern for the environment, and dozens of other aspects of our modern society. So the varied career of Ms. Johnson—who is very much a serious reporter and broadcaster—has added depth and richness to her consumer items on *Market Place*.

Christine Johnson was born in Los Angeles on November 4, 1949, but at age eight moved to Calgary when her father was transferred to that city by Mobil Oil. She was educated at the University of Calgary and Washington State University, where she earned a journalism degree. But unlike many college students who hit only the books, Christine Johnson hit the airwaves and newsprint as soon as she could.

"I was a 'copy boy' for the Oakland *Tribune* while in my first year at University," she recalls. "And I worked on a local show, for an ABC affiliate, hosted a rock music program, an opera broadcast, and produced items on local mayoralty candidates on TV. I was career-oriented, and I never stopped working."

Indeed. By the time she was twenty-one, she was a reporter for a local Calgary radio station (CBR), and by 1975 was doing TV as well as radio reporting. "There were only four of us," she says. "I was one of the first women on the air in that city."

In 1976 Johnson was off to Montreal to work as a radio news reporter during the Olympics. "I liked Montreal *very* much, and made an application to CBC there to be a consumer reporter. I

had always been interested in it." It was her first full-time job, and it lasted a year.

Then politics took a mighty jolt, and so did the career of one Christine Johnson. "The Parti Québécois was elected, Bill 101 was passed, and my beat for a year [1978] was as education reporter on illegal schools—how parents fought against the language bill and similar items." She did a lot of covering of political campaigns as well, and by 1979 she was in Quebec City, covering the National Assembly for CBC-TV.

Johnson became bilingual quickly, assisted by her future husband, a French Canadian, whom

"I was one of the first women on the air in (Calgary)"

she was dating all this time. Then, in 1980, came another career shift, and one that would bring her into direct contact with her present, highly visible position on *Market Place*. "I left CBC to become founding editor of a new consumer magazine, *Protect Yourself*." It had been created by the Quebec government as a give-away, and Johnson's duty was to turn it into a paying proposition, to be sold at a dollar an issue.

By the summer of 1983 it was "quite successful and being distributed across the country"; then *Market Place* came calling, in that very logical place, to replace Joan Watson (who had joined the Canadian Medical Association's task force on extra billing). CBC-TV had known about her, of course, not only from her years of reporting for them, but for her magazine consumerism as well: *Market Place* had used some of *Protect Yourself*'s product-testing on the show.

When Johnson joined the highly successful program, it had been averaging in the area of 1.4 million viewers, and had been on Sunday nights for eleven consecutive years. Suddenly, in the fall of 1983, *Market Place* had a new co-host, a new night (Wednesday), and even a new time (9 P.M.). "It was a handicap," admits Johnson, "and we were up against *Dynasty*!" (An evening soap that you may have heard of.) Yet the audiences of *Market Place* are than ever—a tribute to the powerful interest that the show continues to generate ("one of our shows hit 1.7 million viewers!").

Not that landing such a top job was *all* that has been happening in that very busy life. There was her marriage on June 2, 1984, to André Roy, a labour lawyer in Trois Rivières, Quebec. "We go back and forth between there and Toronto every weekend. We are the Via Rail set!" And it's even

tougher than it sounds, since they each *still* have to drive from Montreal to Trois Rivières, making it a seven-hour journey each way. "We'd been dating and commuting for six years already!"

There is a small apartment in Toronto and a house in Trois Rivières, where Johnson entertained twenty from *Market Place* (croissants and paté) at her own wedding—the guests drove there in a mini-van. (Nine of her brothers, sisters, and their spouses also came, of course.)

If you can cater your own wedding party, you must be pretty good with food, and Johnson is. "People eat very formally in Quebec, and I just *love* to cook a nice meal of many courses for a small group of friends—a soup, entrée, dessert, cheese, bread, fruit. And I like to experiment, never doing the same recipe twice the same way. I use the wok a lot, too."

Back in her Toronto apartment, as you might imagine, it is *not* Culinary City. "I rarely cook for myself. I make a salad that lasts three or four days, or cook a casserole to last the same length of time. And I don't like eating out alone—it's depressing."

In many ways, eating anything at *all* could be depressing for the woman who warns us about pesticide in grains and the dangers of fad diets and exploding pop bottles. "Working for *Market Place*," she laughs, "you are almost afraid to walk down the street!" (No, of course she doesn't smoke, and she fights for nonsmoking areas in restaurants as well.)

"My *major* interest is finding the opportunity to do purely consumer work. *Market Place* is the ideal place for me!" Over a million Canadians happily agree, every Wednesday night.

CHICKEN TEMPURA AND VEGETABLES

INGREDIENTS

2 chicken breasts	2
Juice of 1 lemon	1
1 tbsp. soy sauce	15 mL
2 tsp. sesame seed oil	10 mL
1 large egg	1
1/2 cup cornstarch	125 mL
Peanut oil	
1 garlic clove, finely chopped	1
Green onions, finely chopped	
Assorted vegetables	
Ginger, finely chopped	
Chinese noodles	

INSTRUCTIONS

Remove skin and bone from chicken breasts and slice the meat into long strips about 1/4 inch (.65 cm) wide. Toss the chicken strips in lemon juice, soy sauce, and sesame seed oil. Let the chicken marinate in this mixture from 1 to 4 hours in the refrigerator.

Prepare tempura batter. You can use the commercial mix or make your own: beat together egg and cornstarch, with enough water to make a batter. Prepare a wok for frying by heating a small amount of peanut oil in it. Add a finely chopped clove of garlic and finely chopped green onions. You may remove the fried garlic and onion before adding the chicken. When the oil is hot, dip drained chicken strips, a few at a time, in batter and then fry in hot oil, separating with a slotted spoon. When golden and crisp let chicken drain on metal rack that fits over wok. When all the chicken is cooked, drain on paper towels and keep warm in oven while you stir-fry the vegetables.

This time, add finely chopped ginger and onion to a light brushing of oil in the wok. Keeping in mind the time each will take to cook, add any mixture of vegetables, such as diced onion, cauliflower, broccoli, carrots, mushrooms, and fresh asparagus. Near the end of cooking, add Chinese noodles that have been softened in boiling water and then drained. At the end of cooking, add soy sauce and sesame seed oil to taste.

Serve vegetable-noodle mixture piping hot with chicken on the side (with assorted Chinese sauces, if you like).

It's better than McNuggets and almost as easy to serve!
Serves 2–4

WINE

An off-dry wine from the Loire like Vouvray. You'll need a touch of sweetness to stand up to the ginger and soy sauce.

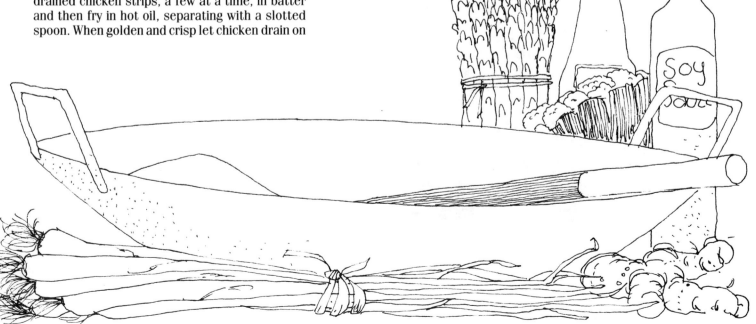

Jonah Kelly preparing an Inuit favourite: arctic char.

Jonah Kelly

This Frobisher Bay announcer tells you how to cook caribou stew

*T*here are tens of thousands of employees of the CBC, and they cover the spectrum of our country: black and white, gentile and Jew, Tory, Grit, and NDP, male and female, from every province and every conceivable background. But when we come to Jonah Kelly, the mainstay of broadcasting in Frobisher Bay, up on Baffin Island, who regales his far-flung audience in both official languages of the North (English and Inuktituk), we are encountering someone *truly* exotic.

After all, what could be more exotic than being born (on October 31, 1946) in an Eskimo hut (a frame made of wood scraps, with a little dome insulated with earth), in an outpost camp near Lake Harbour, on South Baffin Island, on the Hudson Strait? Lake Harbour was one of the first communities established by the RCMP and the Hudson Bay Company back in the early 1900s, and is all Inuit except for the police, some Bay traders, a priest, and an Anglican minister—a few hundred in all.

Frobisher Bay is about 400 miles south of the Arctic Circle. The weather is about eight months of snow and four months of no snow. For about a month each year (the end of May to early July), daylight lasts for twenty-four hours, during which time "you can go outside at 1 A.M. and read a newspaper." Baffin Island is above the tree line, so the tallest things you get up there are "a few shrubs and lichens, and lots of rocks." In mid-August the temperature can soar up to 10, 15, even 18 degrees Celsius. (It was lightly snowing up there on the June evening that this conversation took place.)

Kelly's educational background certainly does not fit into the Canadian norm, much less the CBC broadcasters' norm: his first introduction to schooling was not until the 1956–57 school year, when he was turning ten: "The Anglican minister did Bible study—we studied each other!" He learned *some* Inuit language at that time—"no math"—and it was not until he moved to the bustling city of Frobisher Bay (now about 2,400) in 1958 at age twelve that he truly began his education. "Being a teen-ager, I was a little old for kindergarten," he quips.

But once he got going, Jonah really moved. His first position was with the Department of Indian and Northern Affairs, under Social Services, in a traditionally exotic field: he helped to rehabilitate those who had been in hospitals in the South (that's us), helping them to readjust to the North. Then he did inventory of soapstone carvings for the government. Eventually he hit the CBC—not for the first time, however.

When Jonah Kelly was a teen-ager, the CBC ran a radio dance every Saturday afternoon for the Frobisher Bay Youth Club. Kelly was chosen to introduce records in both languages on live radio, and was heard throughout the town. There was no pay, alas; it was "a free, volunteer thing." But the radio bug had begun to nibble. Then, "one day on a bus, a fellow told me that I should be a radio announcer."

Good advice. So in 1965 when CFFB (CBC, Frobisher Bay) was looking for someone to do teen shows on a more regular basis, Kelly was willing. "My broadcasting career began on a part-time basis," he recalls. And after a few weekends the station manager approached him with a job opening. Two days later he was told to start working for the CBC the following day. "It was a shock for me!" he exclaims. "A brand-new career!" He was nineteen.

The first day of work was December 1, 1965; the starting salary was in the range of $3,000 to $5,000. Jonah Kelly's first job was to establish Inuktituk programming and play a lot of music. He did the midmorning show (9–10 A.M.), and then the afternoon one (4–5 P.M.), "developing programming as I went along. I started from scratch, in the native language only."

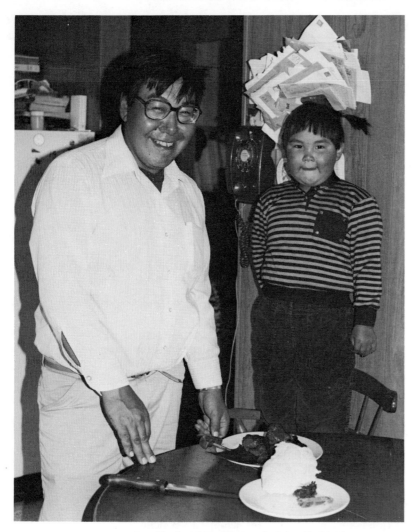

Jonah's daughter Oleepeeka joins Dad in the kitchen of their Frobisher Bay home.

It seems silly, in retrospect: the CBC was already hosting an Inuit-language show out of Montreal, so Kelly would pre-record stuff in Frobisher Bay and send it off to Montreal, which would then broadcast it, via short wave, through New Brunswick and across the world on CBC International. (There are people who speak Inuktituk in Greenland, Alaska, Labrador, Northern Quebec, and, of course, the North in general.)

What is especially interesting and praiseworthy, Jonah Kelly has created a kind of living archive of the North. He has introduced Inuit legends on radio, invites talented people in the area to sing their tribal songs in their language, and much more. "I'm especially proud that I get legends on the air. To Christianity, shamans were a no-no, so the Inuit were hesitant to tell their stories. But I pressed on. Today, we continue to have older people come on the air and tell them." Sadly, none has been translated into English yet. "It would be like trying to translate *Alice in Wonderland* into Inuktituk."

Kelly "found this fantastic woman," Lizzie, whom he married in 1966, and they now have four children, two of each, ranging in age from two to fifteen. As you might well imagine, customs regarding food are rather different up North. "It's not traditional to invite people to your home; people come in for tea or coffee as they wish," Kelly says. "If I hunt and get caribou or seal, however, I call a whole bunch of people over and have a big feast."

Other favourites include rabbit, Canada goose, arctic char, beluga whale, and narwhal ("the unicorn whale with the tusk"). They eat meat and fish raw, somewhat like sushi—but not quite.

Kelly is a tea drinker ("it's easy to make when out hunting; just boil water and add a tea bag—and no chlorine in the water!"). He goes hunting as often as he can, although "gas is very expensive; from $15 to $18 for five gallons, and you have to drive up to 100 miles to get caribou." Snowmobiles are understandably the VWs of the North, with an average of two per person, according to Kelly.

But in between the joys of hunting (and non-cooking), there are those shows that Jonah Kelly broadcasts across the North, in both English and Inuktituk, bringing culture, nostalgia, history, news, entertainment, and warmth into a very cold climate. The next time you hear someone criticize the CBC, remember Jonah Kelly and think of what Northern Services means to tens of thousands of Canadians.

If you really want to be daring, try eating these meats native-style: raw!

ROASTED SEAL MEAT

INGREDIENTS

2 hind quarters of seal meat (about 3–5 lbs.)	(1.5–2.5 Kg)
½–¾ palm of salt, depending on size of palm	½–¾

INSTRUCTIONS

Simmer meat on an open fire in a 3–4 quart (3–4 litre) pail, or boil in water on stove, turning the heat down once boiling occurs. Onions, a dark soup mix, and potatoes are good additions. **Serves: a family**

WINE

Is this fish or meat? I give up: ice water or Chateau Greenpeace.

CARIBOU STEW

INGREDIENTS

3–4 lb. caribou meat (deboned), cut to stew-size pieces	1.5–2 Kg
Oil	
1 medium green pepper, cut in pieces	1
2 sticks of celery, cut up	2
1 onion, chopped	1
1 28-oz. can tomatoes, cut into small pieces	1 795-mL can
1 tbsp. garlic powder	15 mL
Salt and pepper	

INSTRUCTIONS

Brown the meat on both sides in oil, then drain off excess. Add all of the other ingredients, plus salt and pepper to taste. Cook over a low heat until done. Serve with rice. **Serves: a small family**

WINE

Something that rhymes of any hue (as long as it's red). Game needs a super-heavyweight wine from a hot climate like Australia, Sicily, or Portugal.

BOILED CHAR

INGREDIENTS

2 small char (about 2–3 lbs. each)	1–1.5 Kg
¾ palm of salt (small palm)	¾

INSTRUCTIONS

Cut char into 1-inch or 2-inch (2.5 cm or 5 cm) steaks. Put in salted water and bring to a boil, drain, and serve. For a change, try adding chicken soup mix to the water. **Serves: a family**

WINE

A sturdy white wine. If in the Arctic, chill out of doors. (Should you take Jonah Kelly's advice and eat seal meat, caribou, and char raw—good luck! You're on your own.)

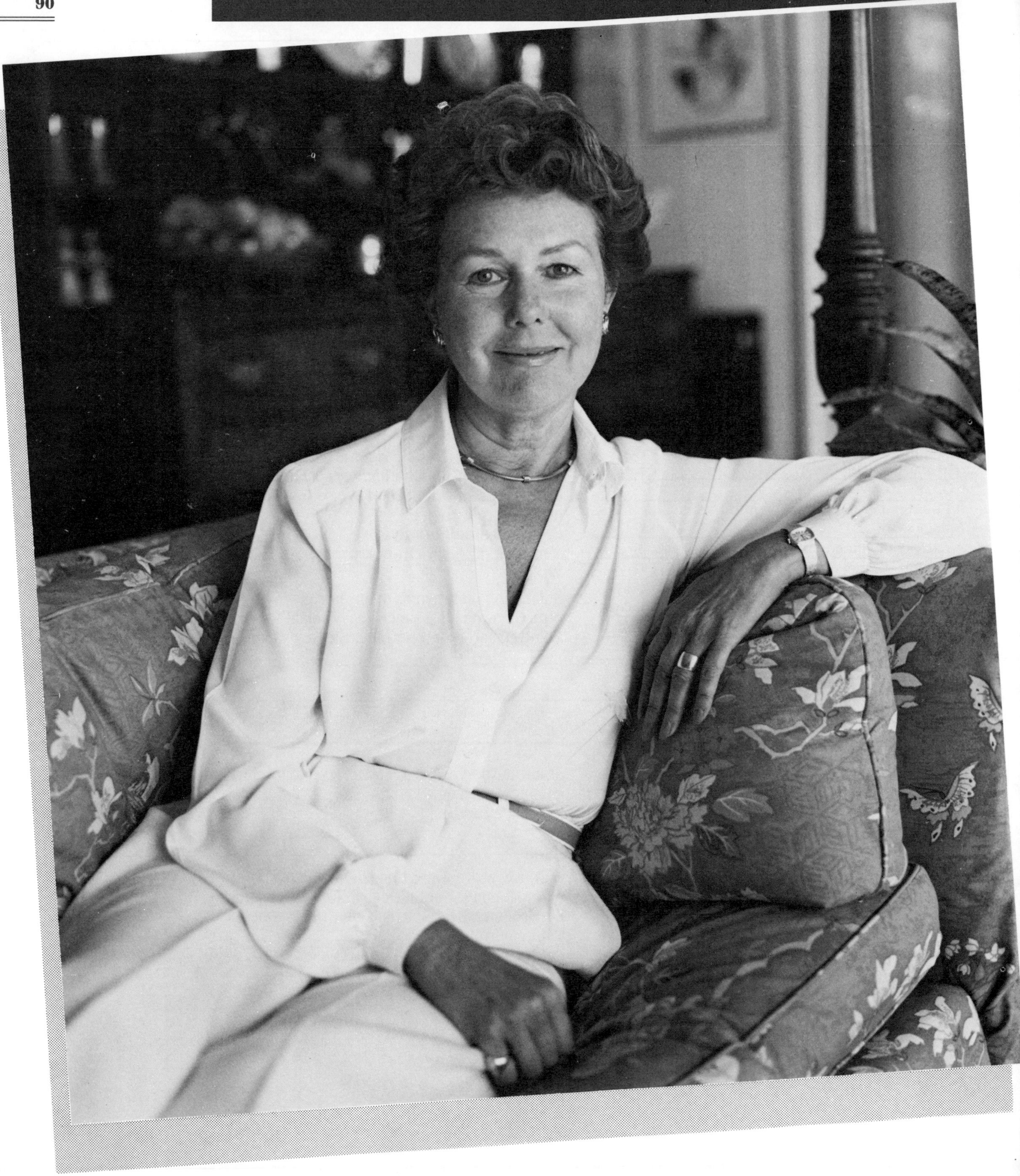

Betty Kennedy

Alligator Stew is not a Challenge to this talented TV and radio personality

*E*very now and then, our neighbours to the south have a survey on "The Most Admired Woman" in the country. And the leaders tend to be Ann Landers or a Supreme Court justice or, more often than not, the wife of the president.

Surely, any similar survey in *this* land would find Betty Kennedy somewhere right at the top of the list. Talk about class! An example: when she moved to Montreal from Calgary in the mid-1950s, due to her husband's business, she met with Herb Capozzi, the program director of Montreal CBC-TV, hoping to talk with him about children's programming.

"He took me down the hall and asked me to interview a man. He yelled at me, 'Take off your hat! Be warm!'" Meanwhile the man she interviewed "kept pitching curves" at the young woman about his divorced wife and a dozen other things. Then the program director looked at Kennedy and said, "We're looking for someone to be interviewer to replace *Tabloid* this Saturday. You interested?"

Betty Kennedy said, "Sure," having never done a TV show before. She did it for the rest of the season. Now that, as I was saying before, is class.

Class runs throughout her life and her remarkable career. She was born in Ottawa on January 4, 1926. Her first job was with the Ottawa *Citizen*, shortly after the war, and it soon led to an assignment to do a fifteen-minute radio show each day for two to three months, during a newspaper strike. "I found that I couldn't write fifteen minutes every day, so I decided to have guests on the show. The station offered me a job when it began to pull in audiences." The station was in Ottawa, and an important career in broadcasting had begun.

Or had it? For Betty Kennedy turned them down, believe it or not. "It never entered my head that it was to be my career!" So it was back to her work at the *Citizen*. But not for long. She was soon asked to work on *Date with a Diplomat* for CBC International Radio, for which she had to do research and broadcast live with Hugh Kemp from various embassies. She laughs about the good old days in that medium: "There was a full orchestra in the studio! That was my real introduction to radio."

Then it was off to Montreal, but she couldn't find a newspaper job, so she got involved "in the fashion end of things." At this time she was married to her first husband, Gerhard Kennedy (of whom she wrote her best-selling and deeply moving *Gerhard, A Love Story*, about their life together and his illness and death in 1975), and

Betty Kennedy and husband G. Allan Burton share a quiet moment outside their home near Milton, Ontario.

> *"There was a full orchestra in the studio! That was my real introduction to radio."*

And then came the moment that led to her face becoming as known to all of Canada as her voice was known to Torontonians. She was asked to be a guest panelist on *Front Page Challenge*, and when Toby Robbins went off to England in 1962 Kennedy was invited to replace her.

Not that her life is all work. She is now married to G. Allan Burton, of Simpson's, and the couple live on a farm about thirty miles outside of Toronto, near Milton, Ontario. They entertain a fair amount: for instance, when her husband was president of the Royal Winter Fair, she entertained over eighty people at home. But there are two other, regular dinners: they invite about thirty neighbouring farmers at Christmastime, and also have a brunch every Boxing Day for another fifty to sixty friends and family.

And speaking of family, there is a large one. Between the two of them, they have a dozen children—Betty Kennedy had four—so it is not uncommon to have dinners for up to two dozen. They might serve crabmeat or cheese soufflé— the latter helped out by the fact that they have their own fresh farm eggs on the compound. And, Betty Kennedy adds: "My husband has a very good wine cellar. He's an expert, and is the chairman of the wine committee of the York Club."

Surprisingly, such a successful couple have no cook. "*I'm* it!" she declares, although, to be frank, she does "modest things that I can prepare quickly." They have a giant freezer, from which she can pull out beef or chicken to be grilled or frozen garden vegetables.

Hobbies include salmon fishing, especially on the Restigouche River, and both Kennedy and spouse are "keen golfers." And there are the honours: She holds several directorships, is an Officer of the Order of Canada, has an honorary LL.D. from York University (both in 1982), and is serving as honorary national campaign chairman for the Canadian Cancer Society (1983–85).

It's hectic, it's nonstop, but it's just what one might expect from a woman who could walk onto a TV set, take off her hat, and be warm—for the next three decades. And three decades more, we all hope.

when they moved to Calgary, she promptly began a weekly panel-discussion show at CFAC in that city. Then it was back to Montreal and her weird introduction to TV interviewing.

At this point we edge toward that for which Betty Kennedy is most famous. After a brief stint in Ottawa, where she researched, wrote, and broadcast a TV Show for a season, she was "told to talk with people in Toronto." Someone said that she should check out CFRB (the most popular radio station in Canada) with an idea she had about "a radio show that could be turned into a TV show." CFRB didn't like her idea, but, fortunately, they "had been looking for a woman for two years."

They found her. Betty Kennedy was soon doing ten minutes every morning (this was in 1959, a quarter-century ago), which soon moved to a one-hour show in the afternoon. Over 25,000 guests have since appeared on *The Betty Kennedy Show*, ranging from five different prime ministers to Jean Vanier, Sir Edmund Hillary, Anne Murray, Lord Louis Mountbatten, and everyone else you could think of. Covering international stories, she has travelled to London, Paris, Rome, New York, Washington, Kenya, Ireland, and China.

CHEESE SOUFFLÉ

Because we have an extended family who often drop in on an impromptu basis, cooking for me must not involve too many hours of preparation. Fresh eggs offer many possibilities. Here is one comparatively quick-and-easy recipe.

INGREDIENTS

2 tbsp. butter	30 mL
2 tbsp. flour	30 mL
3/4 cup milk	175 mL
Salt	
Cayenne pepper	
4 egg yolks, beaten	4
1 cup cheese, grated or crumbled	250 mL
5 egg whites, stiffly beaten	5

INSTRUCTIONS

Melt butter. Blend in flour. Add milk and season with salt and cayenne pepper. Cook until thickened. Remove from the heat and beat in egg yolks and cheese. Return to heat and stir until you have a smooth sauce. Cool mixture slightly and fold in egg whites. Pour into well-buttered soufflé dish. Bake at 350°F (180°C) for about 30 minutes. Serve at once with a tossed green salad.
Serves 3-4

WINE

A good red Bordeaux or Burgundy. If the soufflé falls, pretend it's a soggy cheese biscuit and serve a red wine of lower pedigree.

ALLIGATOR STEW

INGREDIENTS

1 lb. ground round beef	500 g
1 large Spanish onion, chopped	1
2 stalks celery, chopped	2
1 hot yellow pepper, chopped	1
1/2 cup hot ketchup	125 mL
1 pkge. prepared chili seasoning mix	1
1 fresh tomato, chopped	1
1 19-oz. can kidney or brown beans, undrained	1 540-mL can

INSTRUCTIONS

Brown ground beef. Add onion, celery, pepper, ketchup, and chili mix. When mixture is heated, add chopped tomato and beans. Serve with tossed green salad and fresh green peas or green beans.
Serves 4

WINE

Chilled Beaujolais or, if you can find it, chilled Chinon or Bourgueil from the Loire. Invite Dennis Lee to join you—and don't eat this dish with your fingers.

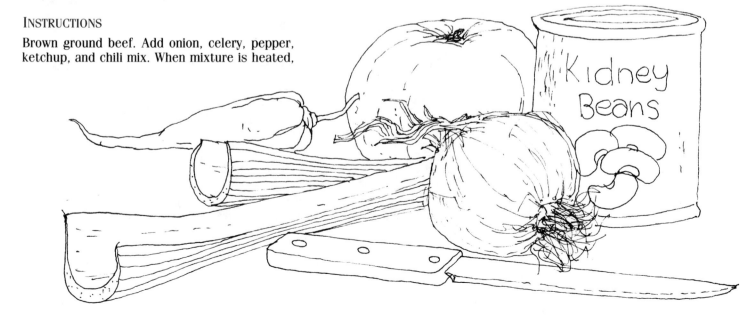

David Lennick

The host of RSVP doesn't extend many invitations for home-cooked dinners

*J*udy Garland spoke of (or was it sang of?) being "born in a trunk." David Lennick was almost born in a radio studio. Not quite—but you'll soon get the idea.

Lennick is, as hundreds of thousands of listeners have probably already guessed, the son of Ben and Sylvia Lennick who, from the late 1940s on, were a fixture on *The Wayne and Shuster Show*, on both radio and TV. (Ben was the bartender in the great Julius Caesar sketch who is asked by Johnny Wayne for a "martinus." "Don't you mean 'martini'?" asks Lennick. "When I want two, I'll *ask* for them!" shouts Wayne. And Sylvia will live forever in Canadian and American memory as Caesar's hysterical wife, weeping over his tragic murder on the Ides of March: "*I told him, Julie, don't go! Don't go, I told him!!*")

But David Lennick *did* go—to the studio, at the age of four tagging along with mummy and daddy to Toronto's run-down (even then) radio studios to watch them perform *At Home with the Lennicks*. "It was a cheap baby-sitter," he says. Indeed, immediately following David's bar mitzvah at the age of thirteen, his parents had to fly down to do *The Ed Sullivan Show* with Johnny and Frank, Sěnor Wences, and all the other greats. (He loved the CBC radio studios—what does a four-year-old *know*?—but recalls going to a Wayne and Shuster hour only once.)

Born on April 30, 1945, David Lennick claims that his earliest *real* acting experience was to be dragged onto a stage with his parents to play the role of a child (type casting! It's dogged him all his life!) in a production of Arthur Miller's *All My Sons*. It was at Toronto's Casino during "one of the rare weeks when it wasn't a burlesque house."

After high school, Lennick went to Ryerson Polytechnical's course for radio/TV arts (to use the words loosely), believing in the profound thought that "radio announcing is the easiest thing in the world." (He had decided at the age of seventeen that that was to be his goal.) He spent three years there without graduating, but he certainly picked up some skills: he was on their radio station half the time, and in all the Ryerson plays for the other half.

He had a summer job at CKFM, then at CJFM in Montreal, and then, "since I couldn't make any money in Montreal," it was back to CKFM in 1968. There followed bits and pieces of theatre and free-lance radio at Toronto's CKEY from 1968 to 1972—"when there was a remote at a Shoppers Drug Mart, guess who was there?"—simultaneously a job at an Oshawa radio station in 1970, where he stayed for seven years, working his way up to program director (CKLB and CKQS-FM): "I was living on $10,000 a year and all the records I could eat."

But, as any good cookbook will tell you, you can't eat records, so David Lennick found himself in 1977 "poor and broke," if not entirely

"I was living on $10,000 a year and all the records I could eat!"

David Lennick and wife Donna liven up meal preparation with a glass of white wine.

"I love Fran's in Toronto; I miss their heavy-duty banquet burgers"

unhappy. (He had happily married Donna Laakso, a dancer and an author, back in 1968, who has published many short stories under the name Donna Lennick).

And speaking of records, how about that amazing collection of his, which rivals Clyde Gilmour's for eccentricity, if not volume? "I began collecting albums as a teen-ager, and about ten or fifteen years ago I realized that there was no reason to be a *snob* about this—I could *use* them to make money." Lennick loves to tell the story about how he walked into CKEY in 1968, leaving his recent bride in the car "with Colonel Sanders," when he discovered that the station was for some strange reason, "giving away its record library." It was January, it was freezing, but it was over an hour later that he remembered the chicken, if not the wife. "I took hundreds of records and went back later for more." Wouldn't you?

Still, all those years were good experience, preparing him for the ultimate low budgets of the CBC: "My boss at Oshawa would let me play anything I wanted. His question was always: 'How much will this *not* cost me?'"

In 1978 he got mad at his boss and knocked at some CBC doors. He did some free-lance on *Mostly Music* and *Morningside* until the big shots at the latter invited him to be a studio director. He was there until May of 1982, at which time the gang at that crucial morning program realized that they had no money in the budget to afford a summer host. "Why don't I quit as studio director, and you can use my salary to pay me as host?" offered Lennick, ever helpful.

His filling in for Don Harron with great aplomb led to calls "every few weeks from Edmonton, asking me to take over *RSVP*." It was an offer he didn't refuse.

Lennick initially left everything at home, including records, wife, and Colonel Sanders. But on April 1, 1983, he moved out to the Alberta capital, where he has been a staff announcer, host of *RSVP*, and host of *Summer Camp* ever since. (If you have missed the latter over the last two seasons, you have really missed something— old radio programs, *The World's Worst Records*, *Three Stooges*, and other such greats. It is, to be frank, a scream.)

"I love the job," is Lennick's enthusiastic comment, proving that his initial interest in broadcasting, if not his belief that it was the easiest thing in the world, was correct. Off the air, David Lennick admits that he and his wife "entertain very little. We're very private people. For sixteen years we've been a good couple by ourselves."

Both cook a little, but neither "is terribly creative," cooking spaghetti, lasagna, barbecuing a lot, and so on. And little booze. As for his taste in restaurants: "I love Fran's in Toronto; I miss their heavy-duty banquet burgers so much." To be fair, he "never ate classy" before coming to Edmonton. "There's La Creperie here that is excellent!"

What is also excellent is Lennick's collection of grotesque songs, including such food favourites as "Hungry Man" ("I know a man/In Alberquerque/Who excels/In baking turkey/So when I crave turkey/I go to Alberquerque/I'm such a hungry man"), "I Like Bananas Because They Have No Bones," and "Please No Squeeza Da Banana," which he describes as "a nice racist '40s song by the Jesters on Decca."

Arthur Black may have his sheepdog, but David Lennick has his short-haired half-Manx cat, Pushkin, which is "very much addicted to cantaloupe, even in the middle of winter, even in the middle of Alberta." It also likes to lick the barbecue grill. "Goddam cat eats better than we do," says Lennick. But thanks to his good/lunatic taste in music, all of our ears are hearing better than ever.

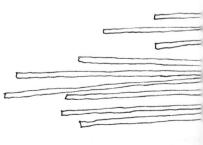

MARVELLOUS SPAGHETTI SAUCE (OR LASAGNA SAUCE) RECIPE

(That started when our meatballs disintegrated in the sauce)

INGREDIENTS

1½ lbs. ground beef	750 g
Cooking oil (olive oil is nice, especially in small apartments)	
1 medium-sized onion (or more if you have a strong stomach and no friends)	1
1 small green pepper	1
6 mushrooms (or as many as desired, including zero)	6
Salt and pepper	
Oregano	
Thyme	
Garlic (powder or cloves)	
Curry powder	
1 28-oz. jar spaghetti sauce	1 795-mL jar
3 bay leaves	3

INSTRUCTIONS

Chop onion, green pepper, and mushrooms very finely. Cover bottom of fry pan (electric or otherwise) with olive oil, and heat to 340°F (170°C). Brown the ground beef thoroughly, adding about half the chopped onion, green pepper, and mushrooms. (It may be necessary to drain excess liquid from the fry pan—otherwise the beef boils and tastes like the CBC cafeteria's Thursday Surprise.) Add salt, pepper, oregano, thyme, garlic (powder is easier), and curry powder to the meat. (Specific amounts depend on your personal taste, or on whether you've been bothered by vampires lately.) Put spaghetti sauce in a large pot on high heat. Add the ground beef mixture and the remaining onions, mushrooms, green peppers, and the bay leaves. Cover, leaving heat high, and stir frequently. When it comes to boiling point, turn heat down to the second-lowest setting and leave it (stirring occasionally) forever. (At LEAST half an hour!) (The sauce is edible once the mushrooms and green peppers are soft, but the longer this simmers, the more magnificent it will be.) Also, if the meat catches slightly on the bottom, this has the effect of sweetening the sauce. (What a nice way of saying don't worry if it burns ...IF, by the way, the whole thing burns/dries up/evaporates because of too much heat—as once happened to me—add a can of stewed tomatoes and a can of baked beans and some chili powder, and fry it up for 30 minutes. You've got one ruined pot and some fabulous chili!) This sauce may be left simmering for up to 2 hours on very low heat. If you cook it in the morning or the night before, simmer it for 1 hour, turn it off, and leave it on the stove. Gently reheat it when you plan to serve it. Remember how many bay leaves you added, and remove them (and hope they're still intact). Serve over spaghetti or spaghettini, or use in lasagna (with grated mozzarella and cottage cheese if you're a Mme Benoit fan). The wine I recommend with this is Szeksardi, or however the heck you spell it.

Serves 4 hungry people, or 6 if you go for the garlic bread and salad. For 2, simply use half the ingredients.

WINE

Copious quantities of Italian red wine—Barbera or Chianti. Serve in tumblers around the kitchen table and get the guests to do the washing up.

Bill McNeil

This native Cape Bretoner enjoys Fresh Air and home-made Codfish Cakes

*S*ince Bill McNeil is one of the great radio announcers and hosts in CBC radio history, perhaps we should begin with the Story That Made Him. It was back in his native Cape Breton, in 1953. The warden of the county jail had been taking prisoners out on hunting expeditions to help him carry back the game, and it struck the great Norman DePoe in Toronto that this was the ideal light piece to end the *National Round-Up*.

So McNeil was asked to cover the story. But what the young reporter discovered was a "medieval jail, with rats, water dripping, and 120 men sleeping in shifts in a building built for one-third that number." He sent his report in and then "sat and shivered. I had *not* done the funny story that DePoe had asked for." That night, the *National* led off with McNeil's exposé of the scandal of a Canadian prison. "I was shocked and proud," he recalls today. A few days later DePoe called and asked if this McNeil fellow could come and be the assistant editor of *News Round-Up* in Toronto.

Of such are great memories made and great careers begun. There have been other highlights, of course, including interviews with Irish President De Valera, Haile Selassie of Ethiopia, and John Diefenbaker (who had "the most piercing blue eyes I ever had sweep over me"). Most notable of all are the seventeen years of *Voice of the Pioneer*, during which McNeil interviewed people "who have known great hardships in breaking the land in the wildest environments that one can imagine from sea to sea. I find it to be pure joy talking with these people who are so totally honest and forthcoming. Most of us wear masks for most of our lives, I find."

Bill McNeil has found out a lot, over the past sixty years, since his birth in Glace Bay, Nova Scotia, on May 30, 1924. The family came from the Hebrides, from which they were sent—Highland Clearance—"on leaky boats to Canada," way back in 1805, speaking Gaelic on both sides of the Atlantic. McNeil's father was a miner, and

after going to St. Francis Xavier for a year, he, too, worked in the mines for seven years to earn money.

"I got married in 1944, built a house, and realized that I had got trapped in the mines, so I sold the house and worked to get away." After the war was over—both the army and the navy rejected him because of his young age—McNeil "looked into radio," pounding at the door of a private station in Cape Breton, continually auditioning there and elsewhere. They kept telling him to "get experience and come back"—but *how*?—until 1949, when the CBC put a station into Sydney, linked with the Confederation of Newfoundland. He auditioned and won a spot there as radio announcer (CBI), at the princely sum of $2,089 a year. "It was peanuts!" says McNeil, who had a wife and a son at the time; he had actually made $300-400 more in the mines.

But then the Big Break came, and he was off to Toronto. He hated the big city at first, missing the Island and old friends, and when he went home the following summer, he almost didn't come back. "But we had changed too much."

Bill McNeil worked with Norm DePoe from 1954 to 1956, eventually took over his job as editor of *News Round-Up*, and was then asked by Harry Boyle to host *Assignment*. The job at the major magazine program—"the predecessor of *As It Happens* and TV's *The Journal*"—lasted fifteen years. A network of nearly 500 reporters around the world would call in their stories, and the show went live every night from 8 to 9 P.M., five nights a week.

"They were *very* exciting years," he exclaims—especially the Centennial Year ("oh man, was I busy!"), during which he flew all over the country, producing *A Centennial Diary*. That year he earned over $50,000—an awesome figure for a free-lancer seventeen years ago. "But I didn't have any time to spend it."

> *"John Diefenbaker had the most piercing blue eyes I ever had sweep over me"*

Bill and Eileen McNeil cel-ebrated their 40th anni-versary on November 29, 1984.

"With radio, it's hard to be anything but yourself. You're either good at it or not."

Fresh Air began in 1969 as a Sunday morning show, and soon became the 6-to-9 A.M. staple on Saturday as well. Cy Strange climbed aboard in 1971: "He's a dear guy to work with." With the show running number one in its time slot in so many areas of the country—including Ottawa, Montreal, Toronto, and Sudbury—McNeil has much to be proud of. That includes his four books: *Voice of the Pioneer* ("a surprise best-seller" in 1978); *Signing On*, about radio in Canada, written with Morris Wolfe; a biography of John Fisher, *Mr. Canada*; and *Voice of the Pioneer*, Volume II, which was published in the fall of 1984.

Bill's wife Eileen worked for the ombudsman of Ontario for five years, but away from their respective jobs, they are "nothing sensational. We're not big theatre-goers or party-throwers. We lead quiet lives and protect our privacy. I'm basically a very shy person."

Perhaps that is why radio was ideal for him. "With radio, it's hard to be anything but yourself. You have no pictures going for you; you're either good at it or not." And Bill McNeil is very good at it—without ever having taken a radio course. And it never seems to stop either, even into his six-ties. "I'm a child of the Depression, and I work bloody hard," he says, taking only Mondays off and working six days a week on *Fresh Air*. "I don't have to chase the buck like I did, but I *still* have that insecurity, the need to hold on. I'm always socking it away, scared that my children won't have enough."

The three McNeil children are all grown; the oldest and the youngest went into the business: Russ McNeil does radio and TV free-lancing and producing; Dawn Marie is an actress; the middle one, Breton, is a management trainee with McDonald's.

McNeil still takes time to share cooking duties with his wife ("I think I'm better than she is, and she thinks *she's* better!"), still favouring Cape Breton food, such as mackerel, herring, salt cod, corned beef and cabbage, and other such local delicacies. Yes, he does smoke—"like a fiend, a large package a day"—but he doesn't drink any-thing stronger than strong coffee.

Reminiscing about his thirty years on radio, he recalls covering Bannister's and Landy's Mile of the Century of 1954, and Hurricane Hazel, when he spent four days searching out houses that had been swept away. "I still remember opening the door of a trailer and seeing a baby floating inside. It was horrible!"

It was. But thanks to men like Bill McNeil, both the grim and the joyous stories of the past thirty-five years from across Canada have become part of our collective memory.

LOBSTER CHOWDER

(From the wharves of Glace Bay)

INGREDIENTS

½ cup butter	125 mL
2 5-oz. cans lobster meat	2 142-g cans
1 7-oz. can finnan haddie	1 198-g can
1 tbsp. vinegar	15 mL
5 medium potatoes, peeled and diced	5
1 large onion, peeled and diced	1
½ pt. table cream	250 mL
Salt and pepper	
Milk	

INSTRUCTIONS

Melt butter in frying pan. Add lobster and finnan haddie. Simmer gently for 5–6 minutes. Add vinegar, simmering for one minute more. Add cream. Boil diced onions and potatoes together in just enough water to cover. When they are done, drain and combine with lobster and finnan haddie mixture. Add salt and pepper according to taste. Add enough milk to cover mixture. Heat and serve.
Serves 4-6

WINE

If you use canned lobster, accompany this dish with a dry white bag-in-box wine. If you use fresh lobster, go the whole hog with a good white Burgundy or Californian or B.C. Chardonnay.

CODFISH CAKES

(From the wharves of Glace Bay)

INGREDIENTS

1 lb. boneless salt cod	500 g
8 average-size potatoes	8
½ tsp. butter	2 mL
2 medium onions, diced	2
2 eggs, slightly beaten	2
¼ tsp. pepper	1 mL
Flour	

INSTRUCTIONS

Soak the cod in cold water overnight. Drain in the morning. Cover again with cold water and bring to a boil. Drain and pull the fish apart into small pieces with a fork, removing any small bones you might find. Peel and boil potatoes. Drain and leave in the pot in which they were cooked. Mash well, adding butter. Add diced onions to mixture. Add codfish, beaten eggs, and pepper. Mash everything together, making sure fish is distributed evenly throughout. Form into 3-inch (7.5 cm) round cakes about 1-inch (2.5 cm) thick. Roll them in flour on all sides and fry in lightly greased pan until brown on both sides. Any remaining cakes can be frozen without loss of quality.
Serves 4 or 5

WINE

Ontario Seyval Blanc or if an all-white meal looks rather boring, add a little colour to the dish with a Tavel Rosé from the Rhone.

Omega Medina

She's as cool as a cucumber (soup) when reporting the weather

*O*ne of the great clichés of Canada is: "If you're *that* good, why aren't you in the States?" For Omega Medina, the weatherperson for the evening TV news of Montreal (*Newswatch*), singer of "O Canada" for the Canadiens (and occasionally for the Expos), and do-gooder around that city, the question read: "If I have so much to offer, why not come to Canada?"

Medina's background is as impressive as her voice. Born in New York City on September 19, 1942, she was the last of four children ("that's why I was called Omega," the Greek work for "last.") She attended the famous Music and Art High School, went to the University of Hartford in West Hartford, Connecticut, and graduated from the renowned Julliard School of Music with an M.A. in 1969. A few years later, she had the opportunity to compete as a finalist in the prestigious International Tchaikovsky Festival in Moscow.

She lived in Milan and Paris—she is fluent in Italian and French—and came to Montreal in 1974. "I knew a lot about Quebec, having spent vacations up here," she declares. Omega Medina wanted to go somewhere to speak French and still be close to her family. "I moved *here* because of the language!" she laughs, recognizing the irony.

It was love at first sight, and it was requited fairly quickly. "I found Montreal wonderful! So *sympathique*! It's a *very* pretty city!" And having been accustomed, from her years in Europe, to living where English was *not* the predominant language, she quickly grew used to "the cosmopolitan flavour here."

Medina's first job in Canada was with an insurance company for two and a half years, followed by an equally long/short stint on radio. "I was the traffic reporter on CKGM. We used to pirate the other radio stations for their reports and call up the police stations. We *all* listened to one another." It was a rock and roll station, but she "loved it. Great people, and an introduction to a whole new world of music." A rather generous statement from a woman more used to singing opera in Russian, German, Hungarian, and Polish. Would that rock aficionados were as generous to the world of classical music.

It wasn't *all* easy, however. "I found the most difficult part was that people rely on their imagination when they listen to you. You have to create a whole world with your voice. They didn't know I was black. I would show up at a gathering and they'd say, 'Where's Omega?' "

Where Omega has been since 1980 has been on the CBC-TV *Evening News* of Montreal, reporting the weather on *Newswatch*, each evening from 6 to 7 P.M. "It happened at a party," she remembers. "I was at the opening of a new restaurant and someone told me that I should apply for a job as writer/broadcaster. They were apparently looking for a woman—and being black, it was two birds with one stone!"

Medina is an announcer who writes her own copy. But she's not a person who could be satisfied with only her daytime duties. She sings and "signs" songs for crippled and deaf children; had

"They didn't know I was black—I would show up at a gathering and they'd say, 'Where's Omega?'"

a music program, *Do You Remember?*, on TV during the 1981–82 and '82–83 seasons, and, as noted above, is one of the two regular singers used before the Canadiens' hockey games. (There were four regular singers, right after Roger Doucet died, but Medina is now 50 percent of the team.)

Omega Medina also works in the black community, giving a talent scholarship of $500 each year at the Miss Black Quebec Pageant. "Some of the women were born here and some are landed immigrants," she notes. "I hate the whole concept, but it's necessary," says the founder of the Omega Medina Canada Award. "You have to be white and French to win the Miss Quebec."

For someone who once sang in a Leonard Bernstein concert for children, it is surprising that she stopped for a full decade; only recently has she begun singing again. She still studies voice as a private student of a lyric soprano.

In the realm of food, Medina is less eclectic. Being single, she cooks mostly for herself, although it's "nothing terribly interesting." There's no time aside from weekends, and she usually makes a casserole and salad and has yogurt with lots of vegetables. She does not eat pork, nor does she drink alcohol or coffee, and she has never smoked ("I wasn't allowed! My father was a Methodist minister. Girls smoke? *Never!*").

A particular favourite of hers is a restaurant called Commensa, in Montreal, a vegetarian place with "*great* food, open seven days a week! It's on Saint-Denis, in the French Quarter." A good plug, Ms. Medina; one can tell that you used to do commercials.

She does a lot of canning in the summer. "I go to the outdoor markets and go bananas! I can yellow beans, green beans, corn, carrots. My ginger pears are out of this world. And I make my own chutney." Unfortunately, that recipe, which includes ingredients ranging from pickled zucchini to onions, raisins, dates, lemon rinds, vinegar, and so forth, would have taken up this entire book. We'll just have to take her word that it's a knockout.

Unlike most of us, Omega Medina is "lucky—my metabolism moves right along." She's five-feet-five and remaining at 120 is easy for her, in spite of her passion for desserts: "Pecan pie à la mode—paradise *can't* be better!" Of course, never snacking, drinking lots of water, and eating solid, square meals slowly probably helps.

With interests in jazz ballet, fashion design—she designs her own wardrobe for TV—swimming, she is as healthy as she looks. And with Omega Medina telling Montrealers what the weather is going to be, it seems as if it's always sunny skies. Now if she can only inspire the Canadiens and the Expos to *play* a little better. . . .

"My ginger pears are out of this world! And I make my own chutney."

CUCUMBER SOUP—VIA BLANCHE

INGREDIENTS

3 medium-sized cucumbers, peeled, seeded, diced	3
1 potato, peeled and diced	1
3 cups water	750 mL
1 cup whipping cream	250 mL
1 basil leaf	1
Thyme	
Garlic	
Salt and pepper	
Paprika	

INSTRUCTIONS

Bring water to a boil, and add cucumbers and potato. Cook till tender. Blend or process until smooth. Blend in cream, basil leaf, and season to taste with thyme, garlic, salt, and pepper. Set aside for 30 minutes to let seasoning set. Chill to serve cold, or reheat to serve hot. Garnish with a pinch of paprika.

Serves 3–4

WINE

Fino sherry, but if you are a teetotaller like Omega, try iced tonic water with a few drops of Angostura bitters.

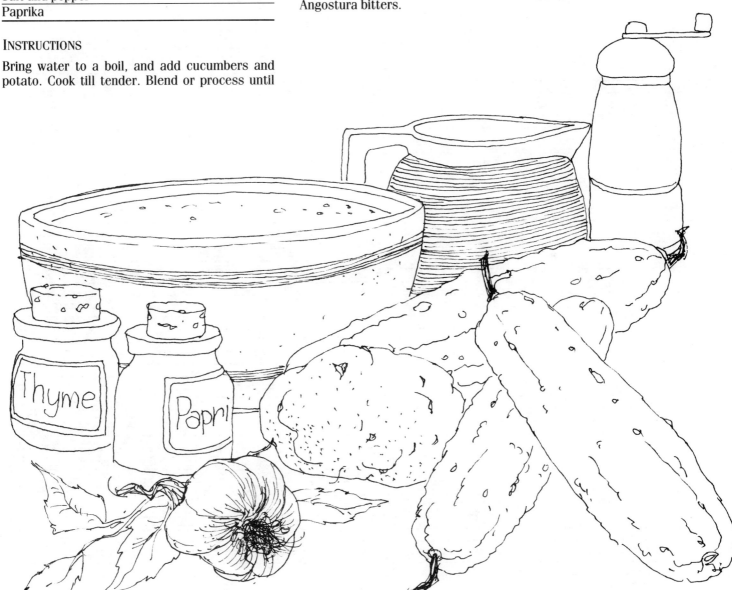

Knowlton Nash

The Anchor Man of The National *reveals his rare taste for raw steak*

As the oldest of the news anchors on national Canadian television—although he hardly looks his years (he was born in Toronto on November 18, 1927)—Knowlton Nash can also claim to have had the earliest entry into the world of journalism. "I sold newspapers on the corner of Bathurst and Eglinton in my native city when I was about ten," he recalls. He also created and wrote a newspaper for his neighbourhood, selling ads to corner stores for gum and candy. "Money had nothing to do with it!" he laughs today.

When it comes to working in Canadian TV news, money *still* has little to do with it. Knowlton and our other newscasters are hardly on welfare, but when we read that Toronto-born Peter Jennings, of ABC-TV in the States, signs a contract for well over $1 million a year, we *know* that the big bucks are *below* the 49th parallel, not above.

Not that Nash is complaining. Viewers with good memories will recall that he has been associated with *The National* almost since its beginning. It was way back in 1956 that he began freelancing on-air for the CBC network from Washington, D.C., being appointed its Washington correspondent five years later.

After only one year of general B.A. studies at the University of Toronto, in 1946, Nash first worked as the editor of *Canadian High News*, a newspaper circulated in high schools, and then zapped around the globe as director of information for the International Federation of Agricultural Producers from 1951 to 1956, where he at least partially satisfied his childhood dream "to be a foreign correspondent."

That came soon enough, with his work for *The National* out of Washington. The stories under Ike, Kennedy, and some of the giants of recent American political history have been kept under wraps before now, but not any longer. In the fall of 1984 Nash came out with his first book of reporter's memoirs, *History on the Run*, where he was finally able to give "the background anecdotes you couldn't tell."

Since November 1978 Nash has been CBC's chief correspondent and anchor of *The National*, and since 1982, he's been married to Lorraine Thomson, the program coordinator of *Front Page Challenge*, who does a lot of producing on her own as well. (Her grandson Jesse often visits them. Coincidentally, Knowlton Nash has a granddaughter named Jesse, the child of his daughter, who lives in Washington.)

Nash knows his reporting, but not his cooking, from the inside. "I may stir, taste, and suggest" to Lorraine, he says. "I'm one to be in the kitchen, sniffing and salivating. I'm *very* fond of good food." He is also fond of entertaining, but the hours of Nash and Thomson mitigate against that. (He is usually at the office by noon, runs home for dinner before five, and then remains at the CBC offices and studios until 11:30 P.M. "It's about a twelve-hour workday, in a *good* week." Bad weeks are when an update is necessary for Western Canada, when he must stay as late as 3 A.M.) "When you work at night, you just *can't* have people over very often."

But they *do* have three major brunches, on Sundays that fall before and after Christmas each year, with up to seventy people at each. "It takes a lot of shrimps and scallops," he chuckles, giving a nice, prime-time plug to the recipe he provided for this book.

In many ways, Nash is the easygoing, relaxed, blond, collected man off the screen that he appears to be *on* the screen. He gave up smoking over fifteen years ago, and never touches coffee or tea. "Skim milk and diet Pepsi are my staple diets," as well as "a lot of grapefruits and melons and bananas." With little butter and no sugar and no salt in his diet, that just may help to explain that youthful appearance. No hard liquor, either: "I drink the occasional beer, and wine at most meals."

His memoirs give "background anecdotes you couldn't tell"

"Journalism is the glue that holds a democratic society together"

Not that there are not times of backsliding. "Coming off a political convention, your food habits are *destroyed*," he moans. "Peanuts! Popcorn! Hot dogs! All the junk food! It's *terrible!*"

But conventions aren't needed for him to indulge in his obsession with Häagen Dasz chocolate chocolate chip ice cream, and his passion for peanuts in the shell. "I love munching cold *blue* steak—meat that has barely stopped moving!"

The world of foreign correspondence helped to broaden his tastes somewhat, even if it only confirmed traditional clichés about foreign cuisines. "The French Embassy in Washington had the *best* food always, and the British always had the dullest!" So who had the most exotic? Why the lobbyists, of course, those men and women who pave the way for good intentions from Senators and Congressmen. "I tried chocolate-covered ants at one of their dinners once," he recalls. *Once*. Ditto for "the salted and dried grasshoppers," which he did *not* like. "When those great big eyes looked at me, it put me off."

Delivering the news, so often horrifying and depressing, has not crushed "the incurable optimism" of Knowlton Nash. "I'd far rather live life expecting the best from people, at the risk of disappointment, than live fearing the worst," he declares. And parallel to his sense of hope and good faith is his belief in the importance of his work: "Journalism is the glue that holds a democratic society together." May Nash continue helping to apply that glue for many years to come, every weekday night at 10 P.M., 10:30 in Newfoundland.

The following dishes can be prepared in less than 30 minutes, are healthy, have low cholesterol content and few calories.

STIR-FRIED PORK TENDERLOIN, CHICKEN, OR SHRIMPS

INGREDIENTS

4 oz. pork tenderloin, chicken, or shrimps	100 g
3 tbsp. soy sauce	45 mL
3 drops sesame oil	3 drops
1 tbsp. cooking sherry	15 mL
2 green onions	2
1 carrot	1
1 celery stalk	1
3 sections broccoli (including stalk), sliced	3
1 handful of pea pods or peas or green beans	1
Corn, mushrooms, cabbage, or whatever other vegetables desired	
4 tbsp. corn or peanut oil	60 mL
¹/₂ cup water	125 mL
1 tsp. cornstarch	5 mL
3 tbsp. soy sauce	45 mL
¹/₂ cup water	125 mL
Rice or noodles	

INSTRUCTIONS

Cut meat into small strips and marinate in soy sauce, sesame oil, and cooking sherry. While meat is marinating, finely chop onions, carrot, celery, broccoli, pea pods/peas/beans, and other desired vegetables. Heat half the oil in a wok. Quickly stir-fry drained marinated meat. Set aside on separate platter and wipe out wok. Add remaining oil and stir-fry vegetables for 1 minute. Add ¹/₂ (125 mL) cup water, cover, and steam vegetables for 5 minutes. Make sure they remain crisp. Combine cornstarch, soy sauce, ¹/₂ cup (125 mL) of water into a smooth mixture. Add meat to vegetables. Stir in cornstarch mixture till thickened. Serve at once on plain rice or noodles. **Serves 2**

WINE

Californian Sauvignon Blanc or Gewürztraminer from Austria or Süd Tyrol, or a B.C. Chenin Blanc. A wine with a hint of sweetness and good acidity is needed to balance the exotic taste.

SHRIMPS'N'SCALLOPS

INGREDIENTS

1 small onion, cut fine	1
2 tbsp. butter	30 mL
2 tbsp. flour	30 mL
1 cup table cream	250 mL
1 cup fish stock	250 mL
1 handful shrimp, fresh or frozen	1
1 handful scallops	1
2 oz. white wine (optional)	50 mL
Pepper	
Pinch of curry or hot red pepper	a pinch

INSTRUCTIONS

Start onion frying in butter. Stir in flour. Blend in fish stock and cream. If desired, substitute 1 can of shrimp soup for the fish stock and cream. Cook for 5 minutes to thicken. Add shrimp and scallops. Season to taste. Add wine. Cook till shrimp are tender, approximately 3 minutes. **Serves 2**

WINE

A good white Burgundy, Californian, or Canadian Chardonnay would complement this dish and boost your morale for the nightly news.

"One of my favourite exercises is 'wokking.'"

Shirley Newhook

Take a Coffee Break and find out what makes Shirley Newhook run

*I*t seems fitting that Shirley Newhook is the host of the extremely popular midday talk show, *Coffee Break* in St. John's, Newfoundland. After all, she drinks it "by the gallon—up to fifteen cups a day—until a nutritionist told me all the troubles that I'd have with my stomach. I call coffee 'the fuel I run on!'" (She is now down to only eight to ten cups a day.)

For a large number of Newfoundlanders, Shirley Newhook is the fuel *they* run on. And that includes Labrador, too. Every year she makes over three dozen appearances, as host/judge/panelist/speaker for many different organizations. Not that *everyone* wishes her and her popular CBC-TV show well: "CTV keeps putting heavy stuff up against me, such as *The Young and the Restless*."

But with such a young and restless woman, do they have a chance? Born on February 27, "some time in the 1930s," in Woodstock, Ontario, she moved with her parents to New York City, where she was raised in that archetypal American city: Brooklyn. She attended Erasmus Hall High School in Flatbush, then went to Brooklyn College for a semester, majoring in English.

But she wanted a modelling career, so Shirley Newhook went to the Barbizon School and worked in the famed garment district of New York as a designer's model, later doing public relations for them.

Then it was marriage, in 1956, to a man who was a sales rep in, of all places, St. John's, Newfoundland. So, reversing the tradition of Newfoundlanders who head down to the States, the young woman headed up to Newfoundland from New York. She came to the Rock in 1961, with two small children in tow, and "for all practical purposes, I was a housewife for nearly a decade." There are three children now, and they are no longer "children": the youngest boy hopes to be a professional rock drummer; the middle daughter is a legal secretary with a law firm in Newfoundland; the oldest works for CBC Newfoundland in TV news.

But from the very beginning, Shirley Newhook was a force in the community. She did service work, fashion shows, commercials. The first job, from 1969 to 1971, was part-time with the *Daily News*, as an assistant woman's editor, followed by the position of features editor. Then it was more free-lance: publicist for the Arts and Cultural Centre, a little music work in "the early days of TV in the province."

The proverbial break came in 1970. While doing publicity for an organization on radio, Newhook ran into someone who told her of an ailing consumer reporter. She got the job and stayed for almost five years. (To give the lady her due, as a teen-ager she had studied voice for more than a decade.)

Then, the bigger break: *Coffee Break*. She got the job in the fall of 1974, which means she is now moving into her second decade there, creating the kind of show on which Joey Smallwood would be delighted to celebrate his eightieth birthday—which he did.

Not that this is *all* she does. In 1978–79 Newhook was the host/interviewer of *Authors*, a regional TV show, and also did two national programs entitled *Atlantic Summer*. Then, in 1980, she was the host/interviewer of *Summer Festival*, consisting of two full weeks of taped shows from St. John's.

She has also been doing some interesting volunteer work on radio for many years. There is a radio station in St. John's, VOWR, which is, in Newhook's word, "unique." At the time of Confederation, in 1949, it was written into the agreement between Newfoundland and Canada that both this and another station would survive,

From the beginning Shirley Newhook was a force in the community

The Newhook family sit down to enjoy a home-cooked meal in their St. John's, Newfoundland, dining room. (Left to right) Christopher, Shirley, Susan, Tracey, and Warren.

"I hate to do the dishes, but I love to cook!"

sponsored by churches in Newfoundland. It's "mostly easy listening," but all the easier to listen to when Shirley Newhook is the host/announcer, every second week for an entire evening: "7:30 P.M. to 11:30 sign-off."

And the other duties? For seven years she has been on the Board of Governors of the College of Trades and Technology of St. John's. She did a stint on the advisory committee of Avalon Cablevision, and sat on the board of the YMCA for many years. She is a member of the committee that recommends the entertainment for the arts centre. And she makes all those appearances across the province for charities, as noted above.

Other broadcasting duties have included 1983's live broadcast of the Royal Couple's visit, when Newhook was co-host for the five-hour broadcast. More recently she spent the summer of 1984 "up to my ears for CBC National doing research on the Papal Visit."

Shirley Newhook entertains "quite a bit," but mostly with close friends. She belongs to a gourmet dinner club with four other couples; they meet about once a month. In the privacy of her own home, she is the cook, and "I love it. I hate to do the dishes, but I love to cook!"

Her favourites? "I particularly like Italian and Jewish cooking." (Her dislikes? "I do *not* smoke, never did, and can't stand it! And everyone in the family smokes!")

Newhook has some restaurant favourites to share with those of you who may be lucky enough to get out to her island: the Act III (in the Arts and Cultural Centre), which serves French cuisine, specializing in fish, and the Fishing Admiral, which "is one of the most popular restaurants here. It has some of the finest fish anywhere."

As does Newfoundland, of course. Listen to Newhook rave about the salmon of her province: "Newfoundland waters are colder, which makes for better salmon. You can pick it up for $3.50 a pound, and lobster for about $4. We can buy it down by the harbour."

And for free, if you are anywhere (except Cornerbrook, for some crazy reason) in that beautiful province, you can flick a switch and get the young and restless Shirley Newhook on your TV. Take a *Coffee Break* from 12:40 to 1:00 P.M., Monday through Friday, on CBC-TV. (And that's Newfoundland time, if you please.)

CRAB-STUFFED HALIBUT

INGREDIENTS

1 8-oz. (250-g) halibut steak per serving, at least 1 in. (2.5 cm) thick, sliced while frozen into 2 thin slices of 4 oz. (100 g) each	
3 oz. flaked crabmeat	80 g
½ cup basic white sauce	50 mL
Lemon juice	
2–3 anchovies, crushed	2–3
2 tbsp. melted clarified butter	30 mL

INSTRUCTIONS

Place one slice of halibut in buttered baking pan. Top with crabmeat that has been mixed with white sauce and a sprinkle of lemon juice. Place the second slice of halibut over the crab mixture. Pour small amount of melted butter over all, and bake in oven at 325°F (160°C) for 20 minutes. Serve with anchovy butter: a mixture of crushed anchovies and melted clarified butter.

Serves 1

WINE

A buxom white Rhone or Californian Chardonnay. The anchovies, the little devils, will overpower less substantial whites.

NEWFOUNDLAND PORK CAKE

(Dark fruit cake)

INGREDIENTS

1 cup finely ground salt pork	250 mL
1 cup hot strong coffee	250 mL
1 cup sugar	250 mL
1 tsp. cinnamon	5 mL
1 tsp. nutmeg	5 mL
1 tsp. allspice	5 mL
1 tsp. baking soda	5 mL
2 eggs	2
⅔ cup molasses	150 mL
3 cups all-purpose flour	750 mL
2 cups golden raisins	500 mL
2 cups whole candied cherries	500 mL
1 cup dates, cut-up	125 mL

INSTRUCTIONS

Place the ground pork in a bowl and pour the hot coffee over it. Let it stand until cold. Then, stir in sugar, spices, baking soda, well-beaten eggs, and molasses. Add all but 2 tablespoons (30 mL) of the flour to the mixture, and mix until well blended. Toss the fruit with the reserved flour until it is all coated. Then add the floured fruit to the batter mixture. Mix well and bake in a well-greased and floured pan. This recipe makes a large cake, and an angel food pan is just the right size. Bake in a slow oven at 300°F–325°F (150°C–160°C) for 2 hours and 15 minutes.

WINE

Have some Madeira, m'dear, with this fascinating cake. But warn vegetarians and Jewish friends first.

Gerard Parkes

The only human on Fraggle Rock *claims the show is a piece of cake*

*I*t's a long way from Dublin, Ireland, to the world of Fraggles, Doozers, Gorgs, and Trash Heaps, but for Gerard Parkes, they were only a few feet away.

I'd better explain: Gerard Parkes, who has "probably done more TV than any other actor in Canada, and that's *not* counting *A Gift to Last* for five years and *Home Fires* for four," was rehearsing for the latter show when he found himself watching the auditioning for *Fraggle Rock*. "I thought it was a rock show!" he says today. The script assistant looked in, saw him, and asked another: "Is that guy an actor?" (It's *very* thankless, working in show business in Canada.) "Would you mind auditioning?" she asked the guy, who *was* an actor.

So Gerard Parkes auditioned—"They had this phony dog there," which is today better known to millions across North America and Europe as "Sprocket"—and he landed the part. He completed the fifty-fourth episode of *Fraggle Rock* in the summer of 1984 and did another dozen for the fall. So much for rock shows.

Parkes made his first audition on October 16, 1924, and over the past six full decades, he has done more theatre, radio, TV, and film than a dozen other performers. He was the eighth of nine children, born to a Catholic family in Dublin. His father worked in the post office, and the youngest boy was shipped off to Catholic schools with the hope that he would attend university. "But I wanted to be an actor," says James Sturgess of *A Gift to Last* and Dr. Albert Lowe of *Home Fires*. So after about two years of high school, while barely into his teens, he was off, first working in linen and cotton factories and eventually, in his early twenties, to a theatre school in Dublin. He attended all the performances he could at the brilliant professional theatres of that tortured, talented country—the Abbey, the Gate, the Gaiety—"seeing everything they did," and he assumed that when he finally went off to London he'd see great theatre. "It was no better!" he exclaims. Spoken like a true Irishman.

And a true Irishman he remained, touring his native island for three years with fit-up companies, which travelled with their own lighting board, scenery, and props on a truck. "We'd do a different play every night: comedies, O'Casey, British plays, *Our Town*." He even played the role of Horatio in *Hamlet*.

"I made no living, but it was great," he says. "I got paid 2 pounds 10 shillings a week, and we paid 6 shillings a night for our digs, which included breakfast, lunch, dinner, and tea. Good digs and good food. But I couldn't save a penny."

Then he was off to England in 1952, but he couldn't get a job at the BBC—"I sounded too Irish"—so he worked first in a passport office, stamping passports, then at Wall's Ice Cream Factory. He got married, had a daughter, Susan, in 1956 (she is a hopeful actress, living in Toronto), and then got a letter from friends who had immigrated to Canada: "You've *got* to come here! They have four or five TV stations."

As he soon discovered, on this side of the Atlantic, there was only CBC-TV—his friends had been picking up the American shows from Buffalo! So while Gerry Parkes had to do phone sales in an office for a time, he soon broke into radio, working with such giants of production and direction as Esse Ljungh and Andrew Allen.

There followed a flurry of stage, radio, and TV work: two or three seasons at Toronto's Crest Theatre ("I got offered $65 a week, and I complained that I had a wife and a kid, so they bumped it up to $75!"). He starred in *Hadrian VII* on Broadway for a year, and received the first Canadian Film Award, today called a Genie, for best actor in Paul Almond's feature film, *Isabel*. He had parts in *Who Has Seen the Wind?*,

He couldn't get a job at the BBC—"I sounded too Irish"

**He received the first
Canadian Film Award,
today called a Genie**

Bethune, *Nellie McClung*, *The National Dream*, *Of the Fields Lately*. There were also juicy roles in *For the Record* dramas. He was kept busy with regular work at the Stratford Festival, the Shaw Festival, Theatre Calgary, Halifax's Neptune Theatre, the Manitoba Theatre Centre, Toronto's St. Lawrence Centre. And, of course, *A Gift to Last*, *Home Fires*, and the only human role in *Fraggle Rock*, co-starring with a phony dog. (So much for W. C. Fields's warning.)

Now divorced but living with a woman, Parkes does *not* cook ("at all!"), but he does enjoy entertaining in restaurants. "I'm funny that way; I seldom have people over." So places such as Toronto's Scaramouche, Cibo, and The Rosedale Diner get his business on a regular basis, which appears to make everyone happy, including his friends. "I make a good Bloody Mary and vodka martini," he says, and confesses to drinking "too much coffee."

When Parkes is not working—and I have *no* idea when that might be—he'll skip breakfast and lunch, and then have a "jolly good dinner." Which must be why, he moans, "I'm lucky! I should weigh 800 pounds, with what I eat!" He has to occasionally cut out bread or beer to remain steady at 175. He adds that he "*should* weigh 160."

After entertaining millions of Canadians with his fine performances for nearly three full decades, Gerard Parkes has recently acquired a whole new, younger generation for an audience with his starring role on *Fraggle Rock*. ("The show is a piece of cake; the best gig I've ever had! The [Jim] Henson associates are *marvelous*, and I only have to work one day a week!")

But, to be honest, he did not become a Canadian citizen until 1968, over a decade after he came to these shores. "What kept me from it so long was swearing allegiance to the Queen!" he explodes.

Spoken just like an Irishman.

These recipes were supplied by one of my favourite restaurants. A special thank-you to Jonathan of Cibo in Toronto.

FUNGHI ALLA PANNA

INGREDIENTS

4 cups whipping cream	1 L
1 lb. fresh mushrooms (sliced)	500 g
2 tbsp. butter	30 mL
Pinch of garlic purée	a pinch
2 tbsp. brandy	30 mL
Pinch of thyme	a pinch
1 cup Parmesan cheese, grated	250 mL

INSTRUCTIONS

In a heavy pot, bring cream to a boil. Let simmer 10 minutes. Sauté mushrooms in butter on a high heat. Add garlic, brandy, and thyme. Add mushrooms to cream. Add cheese just before serving. Goes well with fettucine or papardelle.
Serves 4–6

WINE

To harmonize with the rich ingredients, serve an operatic Italian red wine: Barbaresco (tenor) or Barolo (baritone). Or a mezzo-soprano—Californian Chardonnay.

MARINARA WITH MUSSELS

INGREDIENTS

2–3 doz. mussels, well scrubbed and bearded	2-3 doz.
6 large garlic buds	6
Olive oil	
2 19-oz. cans plum tomatoes	2 540-mL cans
10 leaves fresh basil, chopped	10
10 leaves fresh mint, chopped	10
Pinch of chili pepper	a pinch
Salt and pepper	
3/4 cup white wine	175 mL
2 tbsp. lemon juice	30 mL

INSTRUCTIONS

Brown garlic buds in olive oil. Add hand-crushed tomatoes, basil, mint, chili pepper, plus salt and pepper to taste. Bring to a boil and then simmer for another 5 minutes. Remove garlic buds. Steam mussels open in white wine and lemon juice. Add to sauce and serve. Goes well with spaghetti.
Serves 4

WINE

In keeping with the Italian style, a chilled Soave Classico or, if you insist on a red, choose one with high acidity, such as chilled Valpolicella.

Bill Paul with daughter Erin.

Bill Paul

Readers, take note: this man knows the Market Place

*T*here are times when we look at a child's life and see the future career so clearly that it is almost astonishing. We have, as Exhibit A, Bill Paul, the co-host of the extraordinarily popular *Market Place*, the consumer-affairs show on CBC-TV, since 1978.

In the mid-'50s, while still in his early teens, Bill Paul and some friends actually built a radio station in a friend's bedroom, and they broadcast to the town (High River, Alberta), illegally, every Friday night. "We had two turntables, a tape machine, and a mike."

The petty crooks of the airwaves had put a "helluva big antenna up, and strung it to a tree," so their message of music could be heard by the entire population of 2,000 souls. The highlight of this aural *samizdat* was one Friday night when they had a bad reception and people could only pick up the mini-station from within a block of the "studio." "I looked outside the window, and saw fifteen cars on the street below, with kids outside dancing." Now *that* is Canadian show biz.

Not *all* of Bill Paul's broadcasting has had such impact, but when it *has*, it's usually been on a much larger audience than a group of teens on the sidewalks of small-town Canada. In fact, it has often included hundreds of thousands on both sides of the Atlantic, and, as we well know, over a million every week on CBC television.

Bill Paul was born in Winnipeg, in July, 1940, but since his father was a merchant who "made a hobby of taking dead businesses and bringing them back to life," the lad found himself being bounced from town to town as a child: from Victoria to Drumheller to High River, where he wowed them in the streets, as noted above. It was in Joe Clark's home town that Bill Paul also achieved more legal fame in radio work: in the spring of 1956, when he was in Grade 10, he was approached by his principal to represent his school on a new family station in Calgary. A new *Teenage Saturday Salute* needed a teen DJ, and

guess who took the train to the Big City—seventy miles round trip—and spun platters every weekend for two hours?

Bill Paul attended the University of Calgary (back then, it was called the University of Alberta at Calgary), majoring in Canadian history and earning a general arts degree. And, not surprisingly, he continued to operate for that radio station (CFAC) for free, gaining experience and, probably more important, contacts. After school he did radio work in Drumheller (for $160 a month, believe it or not), Medicine Hat, and then Calgary, where he stayed with CFAC until 1964. (He found time to get married that year.)

"It was a two-hour show, every Saturday morning at 9:30 and we had 20 million listeners!"

At that point CBC opened up a radio station in Calgary and the young Bill Paul happily went to work for them. "The money comes back with sickening clarity," he says. "The salary for announcers at CBC was $6,100 a year, back in '64." He did announcing, music, documentary production, hosted the morning show, played classical music—and did a bit of everything until he came to Toronto early in the Centennial Year.

Rather inauspiciously, perhaps, his first duty was to cover the funeral of George Vanier. Then he travelled 30,000-40,000 miles, covering Expo and other events across the country, and ended the year by covering the Vincent Massey funeral.

In 1968, still relatively new in "the East," Bill Paul began a joyous nine years with *Family Favorites*, a two-way radio show hooked up with BBC London. He was the Canadian host, and there were others in Australia, New Zealand, London, and Malta. "It was a two-hour show, every Saturday morning at nine-thirty, and we had twenty million listeners. My name was more recognizable in Britain than back in Canada!"

It wasn't until 1976 that Paul finally met the host he had spoken with and worked with for so long, talking over transatlantic cable. "You really felt the show *mattered* to listeners," he reminisces today. "It was one of their favourite shows on radio. People wrote in with tears on the page."

But in the world of broadcasting, one rarely sticks with one position exclusively. Over these same years Bill Paul did news and current affairs, *The World at Six*, *Sunday Morning Magazine*, and in 1969 hosted *Weekday*, the first Toronto supper-hour show on TV. Earl Cameron was the news-reader, and a woman named Barbara Frum and Paul hosted the weekday *Journal* five days a week. To this was soon added *Toronto Tonight*.

Paul also got into the world of sports broadcasting as well, but not before doing one weekend of *The National*, *Reach for the Top*, and *Swingaround*, the network quiz show for public school children. By 1974 he was producing and doing commentary for network sports, covering the forming of teams for the Olympics. He covered Innsbruck and Montreal, and recalls being in Dusseldorf as the only radio man there, while TV had ten. "I would go around the world once a month, and it got boring, travelling alone all the time."

No, that is not the voice of a jaded man, but the voice of a loving husband and devoted father. Bill Paul has two teen-aged daughters, and his wife is the vice-president of Corporate Communications at Abitibi Price. "Sharon and I meet in airports often," he laughs. "It *can* be hectic, but it's worked out pretty well!"

What also worked out "pretty well" is *Market Place* which Paul joined seven seasons ago, when Harry Brown went to *Take 30*. It is a busy life since he produces and researches much of what he does on the air.

But there is a private life, too. Every summer he and the family escape up north with their boat: they sail a thirty-seven-foot yawl in Georgian Bay. Cooking is shared, what with a very busy Sharon Paul on the road a lot; "the girls help, too." Favourite foods? "No favourite," he admits. "I eat damn near everything!" Which is why he is lucky to have "a better metabolism than I deserve."

Bill Paul enjoys Scotch and imported wine, and a beer on his boat; he drinks his coffee black. (He gave up cigarettes two decades ago.) But then, working on a show like *Market Place*, one would expect that he would be fearful of eating or drinking anything. But not of broadcasting, of course: anyone who could run an illegal radio station back in the 1950s must have radio waves in his blood. TV waves, too.

"Sharon and I meet in airports often"

BANGKOK CHICKEN

INGREDIENTS

1 3½-lb boiling chicken	1.75 Kg
1 bay leaf	1
1 sprig parsley	1
Salt and pepper	
2 cups long grain rice	500 mL
5–6 medium onions	5–6
2 tsp. peanut butter	10 mL
3 tbsp. oil	45 mL
½ tsp. chili powder	2 mL
4 oz. peeled prawns	100 g
4 oz. cooked ham, diced	100 g
1½ tsp. coriander seeds	7 mL
1 tsp. cumin seeds	5 mL
1 clove garlic	1
Pinch of ground mace	a pinch
½ cucumber	½
2 hardcooked eggs	2
8–12 prawns, unpeeled	8–12

INSTRUCTIONS

Put chicken into large pot with one whole peeled onion, bay leaf, and parsley. Add salt and pepper and enough cold water to cover chicken. Bring to a boil, remove any scum, and simmer gently for two hours or until tender. Remove chicken and let cool slightly. Strain stock through a sieve and use it to cook rice in until just tender. Drain rice and cover with a dry cloth. Remove chicken skin and cut meat into small pieces. Peel and slice remaining onions. Heat oil in large pan and fry onions over low heat until they begin to colour. Add peanut butter and chili powder. Add peeled prawns, ham, chicken, and then rice. Continue frying until rice is lightly brown (use low heat). Crush coriander and cumin seeds and garlic; then add with mace to rice. Salt to taste. Pile onto a serving dish and garnish with cucumber, eggs, and prawns (unpeeled). Serve with a number of side dishes, such as chutney, sliced tomatoes, sliced oranges, sliced green and red peppers with onion rings, pineapple wedges, and/or shredded coconut.

Serves 6–8

WINE

(What did the poor fowl do to deserve this?) There is no wine for peanut butter. Dismiss the wine waiter and call for a six-pack.

GRANNY'S YELLOW PICKLE

INGREDIENTS

7 large cucumbers	7
4 large onions	4
2 tbsp. salt	30 mL
1 tsp. ginger	5 mL
¾ tsp. turmeric	4 mL
Pinch of red pepper	a pinch
3 tbsp. dry mustard	45 mL
½ cup flour	125 mL
2½ cups white sugar	625 mL
2½ cups white vinegar	625 mL
2 cups hot water	500 mL
1 tbsp. butter	15 mL

INSTRUCTIONS

Put cucumbers and onions through a meat grinder or chop coarsely in a food processor. Add salt to taste (about 2 tablespoons or 30 mL) and let stand overnight. Drain well in the morning. Mix together all the spices, flour, and sugar, then add vinegar and water. Boil for 5 minutes, stirring constantly. Add drained cucumber and onions. Boil for another 10 minutes. Stir in butter. Bottle and seal.

Makes 5–6 pints (5–6 500-mL jars)

BEVERAGE

Tap water, unless Granny has been making dandelion wine on the sly.

The Royal Canadian Air Farce

Canada's very funny and talented Group of Five offer comedy and recipes in equal measure

*T*he Royal Canadian Air Farce likes to joke about the fact that they are the ultimate Canadians: Dave Broadfoot is from the West (British Columbia), Don Ferguson is from the (semi-)East (Montreal), John Morgan is Welsh, Roger Abbott was born just across the Mersey from the Beatles' Liverpool, and Luba Goy was born in Germany, to Ukrainian parents. Now if *that* isn't Canadian, then what is?

And if they aren't the longest-running comedy troupe in Canada, and the most popular, on both radio and TV, as well as on stage, then who is?

There is something quite touching about the Air Farce, really, considering how witty and zany they are, and how much needed they are by our traditionally stiff-upper-laugh of a country. To come from so many different places and cultures and all end up in Toronto, on national radio, entertaining millions of others! It is the American/Canadian dream come true, and it's kind of wondrous that they did come together.

Since there are five of them I'll take them one at a time: their recipes are at the end of this lengthy chapter.

LUBA GOY, one of the finest female comics in Canada, was born in one of Europe's most dreadful locations: a "work camp" of the nonpaying variety, after the war, on November 8. (The year isn't important. Let's just say that she *must* be over thirty; her son is almost ten.) Goy's Ukrainian parents met in the camp, left when she was barely a year old, and went to Belgium, where her mother became a cook for a wealthy family in Luxembourg. Her father used to tour with a large choir in Europe, and her mother also worked in a dance troupe, so there was certainly a lot of stage talent in those genes. By the time she was five, Luba Goy was in Ottawa, speaking English, Flemish, Ukrainian, and "a little French."

"My dad was a natural comic who wrote satirical pieces, in both Belgium as well as this country," Goy recalls. "The same sort of stuff I do now." But he died when Luba was still a child. Her mother later remarried, and provided the future radio and TV personality with other siblings, with whom she is very close.

Each year the National Theatre School of Montreal holds auditions across the country and chooses only six performers. The year Goy auditioned, she was chosen. Then she was hired by Jean Gascon, to work at the Stratford Festival. "I was very fortunate," she declares. The National Arts Centre had just opened, and she found herself acting in such plays as *The Hostage* and *Empire Builders* at the NAC, as well as on the Third Stage of Stratford.

Then occurred that special moment which each of these five inspired maniacs had to experience: the chance to join a comic group. After auditioning for Marion André in Montreal, she was urged to audition for The Jest Society, an improvisational troupe that was doing some good stuff, back in 1973. She joined them the same year that Don Ferguson did, and they developed into The Royal Canadian Air Farce on CBC Radio.

Not that she has done *only* the RCAF. Her work on CTV's *Bizarre* has been seen across

Luba Goy

Luba Goy with son Gabriel

In Canada, Morgan was a journalist for about a decade, editing for a time *Montrealer Magazine* (rest in peace), which he describes as "the *Punch* of Canada." Then, in 1966, he began to make use of the comic talents that hadn't been fulfilled in the classroom, newsroom, or racetrack pits, co-creating *Funny You Should Say That*, the CBC radio comedy series. He then went on to help form The Jest Society, and eventually the Air Farce.

Other things also have attracted his skills. He has written for a number of radio and TV shows; he is the major writer of the RCAF; he even hopped back to England in 1976 to star in his own BBC Radio series, *It's All in the Mind of John Morgan*.

Morgan is happily married with two children, seventeen and nine, who joyously spend much of their summers—when not performing for eight weeks with a theatrical show, as they did in 1984 at the Young People's Theatre—above a restaurant in Bala, Ontario (about 120 miles north of Toronto, near Gravenhurst). His wife used to run the restaurant; now they just live above it.

"My wife is a darned good cook," says the noncooking comedian. Not that he doesn't enjoy eating out, such as at the Leaning Tower of Pisa (or is it Pizza, he asks), in Montreal, where they purportedly "do a *great* ravioli." Maybe so. But can they do a Pastor Quagmire, or an Amy de la Pompa, as Morgan does, on Air Farce?

North America, as has her lovely, warm teaching of the world of computers on *Bits & Bytes*, an educational series put out by TVOntario.

As for the world of food, Goy is a *maven*, to use a non-Ukrainian word. "I *love* entertaining! I give garden parties and have *lots* of people over—dozens! I make sure some bring their children and babies." And she does all her own cooking for them, too.

Luba Goy loves "international cuisine," which is not surprising, considering her background. And, because she *loves* to eat, "I feel like a five-foot butterball all the time."

But she does not look like one. Whether it is her tea-drinking or the fact that she makes desserts for others but doesn't eat them herself, she remains in rather good shape. Maybe the secret is running around with four crazed men all the time.

"I feel like a five-foot butterball all the time!" *(Goy)*

JOHN MORGAN is the other "ethnic" of the group, if one can call a Welshman that. Born on September 21, 1930, in Wales, he did not come over to Canada until 1957. The years between were certainly strange ones—he studied physical education and English at the University of Wales—then served in both the classroom and on newspapers (as a journalist) for a number of years. He also spent time "hoboing around auto racetracks, working in the pits. It's the national mining instinct of the Welsh!"

John Morgan

If **DAVE BROADFOOT** isn't Canada's most beloved comedian, then he certainly is closer to it than the head of the New Democratic Party (that's Broadbent), a zillionaire folksinger (that's Lightfoot), or a popular oral historian (that's Broadfoot, all right, but Barry).

Born in North Vancouver, on December 5, 1925, Broadfoot is the one with the most experience of the five, having decided way back in 1952 —over thirty years ago!—"to become a professional comedian."

Not that his family would have wanted it. They were "extremely religious"—Baptist fundamentalists—which meant that he wasn't able to see any theatre until he finally left home after dropping out in Grade 9 to join the merchant marines, "sailing all over the world." (His three sisters are all missionaries, currently in Bolivia, Japan, and Victoria, B.C. Of course, one *could* make an argument for comedy as a kind of missionary work, couldn't one?)

After seeing the world, and theatre, Broadfoot came home and went into the clothing business, "where I learned to be an actor—I memorized lines between customers." He acted in many different little community and local theatres in British Columbia, and even worked in a Jewish resort for three years up in Muskoka, north of Toronto. "I was one of the few gentiles there, and I loved it. That audience became my fans."

The first things Broadfoot did on stage were comedy, and he was actually "surprised that I had intuitive timing, which is so crucial to successful comedy." Furthermore, "the only satisfaction was to hear the laughter of the audience," so he "developed an act," in order to continue in the medium he loved so much. The first paid job was at the Sirocco Night Club in Victoria.

In 1952, he headed for Toronto, where he auditioned for television, which was barely starting. The next year he made it into a show that became a venerable institution, *Spring Thaw*, on which he happily laboured over the next few years. It was in Montreal, nearly two decades after he arrived in "the East," that he and Morgan got together: "I was doing *Squeeze*, a cabaret, and John was doing *Funny You Should Say That* and was the regular on *Comedy Cabaret* on TV."

The magic synthesis didn't happen overnight. Broadfoot never worked with The Jest Society, but when it was later running at the Poor Alex in

Toronto, he was invited aboard as a guest. By 1973 he was one of the principals. "It was live audience! I *liked* that," says the once and future stand-up comic.

Off the stage, Broadfoot has a wife, Diane Simard—"she's my manager"—and a fourteen-year-old daughter. He doesn't cook: "The fact that my wife is a gourmet chef makes me feel superfluous and inadequate." His favourite food is sushi (at least you don't have to cook that), and his taste in restaurants runs toward Honjin, Sasaya, and Monami, all Japanese, all in Toronto. He enjoys drinking such beverages as red wine and vodka (although not necessarily together. That's called a Cariboo, and he enjoys that as well).

When asked about "food humour" in his work, the man who gave the world Bobby Clobber (the stunned hockey player), Sergeant Renfrew of the Mounted (the stunned RCMPer), and the Member for Kicking Horse Pass (the stunned MP), he recalls a not-so-stunned sketch from 1983. Each Air Farce member had to impersonate what they ordered in a restaurant, Chez Charade. "Roger wanted fish, so he swam on his chair. Luba went into her chicken act. Poor John had an unexpected heart seizure, and the waiter kept trying to interpret what he appeared to want, while he was dying."

And Dave Broadfoot? He stood up and walked out in a rather strange manner, prompting the waiter to say something like, "Your snails will be right out, monsieur!"

Very funny, Broadfoot.

"The only satisfaction was to hear the laughter of the audience" (Broadfoot)

Dave Broadfoot

The Royal Canadian Air Farce takes a break between rehearsals at the Bayview Playhouse Theatre in Toronto. (Clockwise from bottom right) John Morgan, Don Ferguson, Roger Abbott, Dave Broadfoot, and Luba Goy.

"I love restaurant sketches. Restaurants are very formal, like a church..." (Ferguson)

DON FERGUSON, who was born on May 30, 1946, in Montreal, had the most traditional of all the backgrounds of the Air Farceurs. He graduated from Loyola College in Montreal with an Honours B.A. in English and then almost immediately slid into writing and performing comedy. He had played the trumpet, edited the newspaper, and worked in theatre production back at Loyola; but he ended up in a far more lucrative situation with The Jest Society following brief stints in radio operations, audio-visual producing, and photography.

Ferguson is married to a talent agent who rather kindly handles her spouse's commercials, Dave Broadfoot's commercials, and Luba and Roger for just about everything. (It's called First Artists Management, in case you wish to get hold of these people for your wedding, bar mitzvah, or confirmation.)

Both Fergusons are good cooks, but most of his time is spent with the Air Farce, which recently completed eleven years on Canadian radio—twenty-six weeks a year and thirteen weeks of repeats, for thirty-nine weeks in all. During the summer of 1984 Ferguson and Abbott hosted a show called *Air Farce Presents Comedy Classics* in their regular slot on CBC-AM. "So we were on for fifty-two weeks that year!" he exclaims.

Don Ferguson is a nonsmoker, a Japanese food lover, and a fan of The Grill in Three Small Rooms in Toronto. And since he has lived in Italy with his Italian-American wife, he is rather obsessed with that wonderful cuisine, as well.

This leads me to *his* favourite food sketch, which was in their summer 1984 stage show. John and Luba are customers in a good French restaurant, listening to Don describe the food. They request lamb. "I am sure that our lamb won't mind." They are troubled. "How about the trout? "I will personally slice open the soft underbelly..." "Spareribs?" "I'll make sure that the pig is dead...." They finally end with our French waiter Ferguson describing Toronto tap water, which *really* turns the customers off.

"I *love* restaurant sketches," says the man

The initial work on the airwaves was less creative, at least in the writing and performing sense. From 1965 to 1970 Abbott was a technical operator, then did promotion, then music programming, and finally, "I ended up as an operation manager."

After he quit to go free-lance, he fell into The Jest Society. "The notion was that these were a bunch of people who weren't actors, and were not embarrassed to make fools of themselves. It was May of 1970 when I joined them, and I've been making a fool of myself ever since!"

Abbott is the only single one of the group (albeit Ms. Goy is divorced). "I entertain, but eight is my maximum, since I can seat only six comfortably. I *do* cook. It took a long time to learn, but I really enjoy it." Unfortunately, Roger Abbott is "one of those cooks who can't concentrate on more than one thing at the same time," so he tends to fall into a self-laid trap. "Always thinking that it will be easier than it is," he invites people to come at 7:30 P.M., buys his groceries from 5:30 to 6:30, and never has the food ready and on the table before 8:30 or 9. Be warned, should you ever get invited.

Thank heavens he doesn't have to cook for his fellow-farceurs, though, or The Royal Canadian Air Farce might *never* get on the air on time. And that would be a national calamity, as we all know.

"It was May of 1970 when I joined them, and I've been making a fool of myself ever since!" (Abbott)

who sounds more like Trudeau and Mulroney than Trudeau and Mulroney do. "Restaurants are very formal, like a church. So certain things are not supposed to happen..." Which is as good a definition of comedy as you'll find in a long time.

ROGER ABBOTT met Don Ferguson at the age of twelve, in Montreal, when they both tied for fifth place for a scholarship to Loyola. Since there were six scholarships, it was a positive meeting. But hardly an inevitable one because Abbott was born in Birkenhead, England (on July 10, 1946).

In 1953, he came to Montreal with his family, tied with Ferguson a few years later, but unlike his future partner did only one and one-half years at the college. "Instead of attending classes, I did theatre promotion, performing, newspaper writing, radio." He got a job with CKGM in Montreal, having quit university for a year. The year stretched into nearly two full decades. "Nineteen years later, I'm still here," laughs Abbott, who is, indeed, still on radio.

Don Ferguson

Roger Abbott

STRAWBERRY SOUR CREAM TORTE

(*Luba Goy*)

INGREDIENTS

12 large eggs (or 14 small), separated	12 (14)
2 cups sugar	500 mL
2 cups sifted cake flour	500 mL
4 tsp. baking powder	20 mL
½ tsp. salt	2 mL
Juice 1 lemon + enough cold water to make ½ cup	125 mL
1 qt. strawberries	1 L
4 cups thick sour cream	1 L
½ cup sugar	125 mL
2 tbsp. gelatin	30 mL
4 tbsp. cold water	60 mL
1 pt. whipping cream	500 mL
¼ cup icing sugar	50 mL

INSTRUCTIONS

Beat egg whites with 1½ cups (375 mL) sugar until they form soft peaks (not too soft). Beat egg yolks with remaining sugar until lemon-coloured.

Into the yolks, add flour, baking powder, and salt alternately with the lemon juice. Fold egg yolk mixture into beaten egg whites. Divide batter into two 11-inch (27-cm) spring-form pans. Bake at 350°F (180°C) for 35–40 minutes. Cool. Slice each layer in half. Process strawberries until coarsely cut. Combine sour cream, sugar, and strawberries. Dissolve gelatin in water. Heat over hot water until clear. Fold into sour cream mixture. Fill layers of cake with strawberry filling. Whip cream until stiff. Beat in icing sugar during the last few minutes. Frost cake with whipped cream mixture, and decorate with strawberries.
Serves 12

WINE

A luscious sweet Sauternes or Barsac served well chilled. If on a diet, forgo both dessert and wine and have a banana.

LANCASHIRE HOT POT

(*Roger Abbott*)

INGREDIENTS

2 lbs. stewing beef	1 kg
2 tbsp. vegetable oil	30 mL
1 cup water	250 mL
1 medium onion, chopped	1
Salt and freshly ground pepper	
6 medium potatoes, sliced	6
6 medium carrots, sliced	6
1 large onion, sliced	1
1 tbsp. cornstarch	15 mL
2 tbsp. cold water	30 mL

INSTRUCTIONS

In a large saucepan, sauté beef (¼ at a time) in hot oil until browned. Remove to a dish in a warm place. After all the beef has browned, add water and scrape down sides and bottom of pot. Return meat to the pot. Add chopped onion, and season. Bring to a boil, reduce heat, cover and simmer, stirring occasionally, for 1¾ hours. Remove meat from juices when it has cooled. In a greased 10-cup (2.5-L) casserole dish, arrange a layer of potato slices, then a layer of carrots and onions, and finally a layer of beef. Meat juices can be poured over each layer. (If desired, thicken juices with cornstarch mixed with 2 tablespoons water.) Cover casserole and bake at 325°F (160°C) for 1 hour, until vegetables and meat are tender.
Serves 7–8

BEVERAGE

Newcastle Brown Ale at room temperature. Serve it in liberated pub glasses and talk soccer.

P.E.I. TREASURES

(*Dave Broadfoot*)

INGREDIENTS

2 lbs. mussels, cleaned	1 Kg
2 oz. unsalted butter	50 mL
2 tbsp. green onions, chopped	30 mL
2 oz. dry white wine	50 mL
Juice 1 lemon	1
1 cup whipping cream	250 mL
1 sweet apple, peeled, thinly sliced	1
Salt and pepper	
2 tbsp. fresh chives, chopped	30 mL

INSTRUCTIONS

Get out into a muddy cove when the tide is out. Dig out at least 2 pounds (1 Kg) of mussels from the mud. Scrub all mussels under cold running water with a wire brush or stiff bristle brush.

Melt butter in a pan. Add green onions and simmer lightly. Add lemon juice, wine, and mussels. Bring liquid to a boil and then lower heat to simmer. Keep cover on your pan until all mussel shells are open (3–5 minutes). Remove mussels from pan. Add cream, apple slices, and seasoning to liquid in pan. Reduce over medium heat until the sauce thickens. Place mussels in a deep soup plate. Add chives to sauce and pour over mussels. Serve. If the other person doesn't care for it, you get twice as much—so you can't lose. **Serves 2**

WINE

After all that hard work you deserve a good bottle of chilled Muscadet or Chablis. If no other dish is served, round off the meal with a *trou Normand*—a small glass of Calvados.

TUKTOYAKTUK CURRY

(*John Morgan*)

INGREDIENTS

Rice
Curry
Mayonnaise
Sultana raisins
Chopped pineapple
Roasted peanuts

INSTRUCTIONS

Boil rice until appropriately ripe. Allow to get cold. Make a paste of curry and add mayonnaise to taste. Throw the sultanas, pineapple, and peanuts into the cooked rice. Then add curry-mayonnaise paste and mix thoroughly with rice. Serve cold or freeze and serve on a stick. Keeps the flies off your lips.

WINE

Wait for a passing St. Bernard dog. Relieve him of the wooden cask around his neck and consume contents before embarking on this recipe. (What a terrible thing to do to a sultana!)

EASY BERMUDA BARBECUE SAUCE

(*Don Ferguson*)

INGREDIENTS

1/4 tsp. chili peppers	1 mL
1 clove garlic, minced	1
1 tbsp. dry sherry	15 mL
2 tbsp. brown sugar	30 mL
1/8 tsp. ground ginger (optional)	a pinch
1/4 cup ketchup	50 mL
Salt and black pepper to taste	

INSTRUCTIONS

Combine all the above ingredients. Brush on chicken, ribs, chops, steaks, hamburgers.

BEVERAGE

Double the amount of sherry called for in the recipe, separate into two glasses. Consume both and substitute wine vinegar in the mixing bowl.

Lister Sinclair

The host of CBC Radio's Ideas has more than a few of his own

*T*o introduce the very remarkable radio and TV personality Lister Sinclair, let me borrow the words of Fred Davis, when he introduced our subject some years ago (before honouring him with the John Drainie Award at the ACTRA presentations): "mathematician, linguist, poet, playwright, philosopher, naturalist, film-maker, sports enthusiast, racing-car buff, birdwatcher, and compulsive teacher." That's quite an introduction!

The origins and impressive educational background of Sinclair will come as little surprise to those thousands of us who have been moved and inspired by his wonderful studies of music on *Morningside* ("such a great opportunity to talk to a great number of people") or, more recently, his fine commentaries on *Ideas*. He was born in Bombay, India, in 1921, the son of Scottish parents, and was educated in London, England. He attended St. Paul's, "the first Renaissance school," he eagerly relates. "It was founded with the idea of bringing the Renaissance to England, so we studied Latin, Greek, French, and German." Sinclair also did a lot of acting at St. Paul's, and it served him well when his family moved to Vancouver shortly before World War II broke out.

He attended the University of British Columbia, where he met and befriended one Pierre Berton, with whom he wrote for *Ubyssey*, the university newspaper. After receiving a degree in math and physics at UBC, Sinclair went off to the University of Toronto in 1942, studying for five years and ending up with a master's. He taught math at the U. of T., commenting that "by far the *best* way to learn a subject is to give a course in it!" (He has since taught at Toronto, UBC, York University, and, indeed, over radio and TV for four decades.)

Toronto, of course, was a marvellous place to continue one's acting career, which he did, and he

shared his theatrical knowledge as well, teaching in Lorne Greene's famous Academy of Radio Arts in the late 1940s.

"I'm a very good impersonator, doing short character vignettes, and I'm a very good reader.

But I'm *not* a good actor," he confesses. So it was not surprising that acting soon gave way to playwriting. He began penning original works as early as 1944, while working on his M.A. at U. of T., and in a short time his plays were being produced under the leadership of Andrew Allan,

"The best way to learn a subject is to give a course in it!"

on CBC radio. They were also performed at Toronto's seminal Jupiter Theatre (including *Socrates* and *The Blood Is Strong*), and, earlier, at Mavor Moore's important New Play Society (*Man in a Blue Moon*, among others).

Since the late '40s Sinclair has been one of the mainstays of the CBC, on both radio and TV, and on both sides of the microphone/camera—as writer, producer, director. And more: he was one of the major organizers and administrators of the Association of Canadian Radio and Television Artists (ACTRA). He served as radio panelist on *Court of Opinion* for two dozen years. He did a number of award-winning films for the National Film Board, including *Opera School* and *Man in the Peace Tower*.

At CBC-TV, Sinclair was responsible for some of the finest science shows and dramas to come out of the corporation in the 1960s and 1970s: the *Man at the Centre* series, including studies of Darwin and Thoreau; a series on *The Long-Haired Heroes*: Berlioz, Liszt, and Wagner; *The Nature of Things*; major documentaries on Shakespeare and Shaw; *Ambush at Iroquois Point*; six science programs for TVOntario. And he has received dozen of awards, including honourary doctorates, the Sanford Fleming Medal, and the revered Peabody Award for his superb radio documentary on the year *1905* for *Morningside*, back in 1982. (The Peabody is radio's equivalent of the movies' Oscar, and probably a lot more meaningful, in terms of talent and skill.)

There have been some hiatuses in his writing-broadcasting career, such as a lengthy stint in Ottawa, as vice-president of Program Policy and Development, and executive vice-president of the CBC, in the early 1970s. Of this period Sinclair wittily comments, "There are *no* glowing moments for administrators." Still, he does acknowledge that those years have been helpful in preparing for 1978–82, when he was the president of the Canadian Conference of the Arts.

When I brought up the subject of cooking, his immediate response was: "I like cooking. I have views on cooking. I suppose it's having a mathematical background and natural-history interest. For instance, there are many varieties of oil and vinegar salad dressing, so it's not helpful to call them *all* 'French dressing'—to cry, 'I put tarragon in mine!' or, 'In mine, I use Dijon mustard.' There is a *standard* in French dressing, whether in Escoffier or Julia Child: three to one, oil over vinegar. *That* is what French dressing *is*!"

Obviously, Lister Sinclair has very definite ideas about food. As he says: "I went to boarding school, so I can eat *anything*!"

As for hobbies, he gives the reply that one would expect him to give: "Natural history. But in a sense, everything that I take up, I do with great intensity." Meaning, of course, that if one feels passionately about something, it's too serious to be labelled merely "a hobby."

"I like birdwatching because there are no deadlines. If you go out and see nothing, that's interesting, too. You don't have to come back with a result *every* time."

But in Lister Sinclair's broadcasting and writing career, he clearly *has*.

"I went to boarding school, so I can eat anything!"

LAMB CHOPS CHAMPVALLON

This is a simple, elegant, and high-class casserole designed by the great Escoffier, Edward VII's chef. It's a dish fit for a king; especially a king with perfect taste.

INGREDIENTS

4 double loin lamp chops, well trimmed	4
Vegetable oil	
2 medium-sized onions, diced	2
1 clove garlic, chopped	1
1 cup chicken or veal stock	250 mL
1/3 cup white wine	75 mL
1 bay leaf	1
Salt and pepper	
4 medium-sized potatoes, thinly sliced	4
Pinch of thyme	a pinch
Parsley, chopped	

INSTRUCTIONS

Brown chops in the oil. Place in a casserole. Brown the onions along with the garlic in the same oil and add to the casserole. Add the stock, wine, bay leaf, salt, and pepper. Top with a layer of potatoes. Sprinkle a little thyme and parsley on top. Cook in oven at 350°F (180°C) for 40 minutes (covered), then for another 20 minutes (uncovered). Brown for five minutes.
Serves 4

WINE

The red wines of Bordeaux were made to accompany lamb, especially when grilled. In casserole form, your choice need not be Chateau Lafite, but a good sturdy Bordeaux blend.

PORK CHOPS WITH BASIL

Escoffier was rather haughty about pork. He called it a domestic meat, fit only for bourgeois households. The Chinese, whose cuisine is the equal of the French, would not agree with him. Besides, I must have bourgeois tastes, mixed in with all the rest, because I love pork chops. This recipe has an Italian flavour about it.

INGREDIENTS

4 pork chops, thick and well-trimmed
Flour
Garlic salt
Olive oil (*not* vegetable oil)
Fresh basil, chopped
Wine (Marsala, Madeira, or sweet sherry)

INSTRUCTIONS

Dredge chops in the flour and garlic salt. Brown them on both sides in a minimum amount of oil. Place them in a casserole, sprinkle with basil, cover, and bake in oven at 300°F (150°C) for about 1 1/2 hours, or until tender. Now uncover them, add 1/3 cup (75 mL) wine, and cook for another 10 minutes, basting every so often.
Serves 4

WINE

To complement the sweetness of the meat you can try a Spätlese from the Rhine or a Vouvray from the Loire—unless, like Lister, you prefer the heavier taste of fortified wines.

David Suzuki with wife Tanis Cullis and daughters Severn and Sarika.

David Suzuki

It's in The Nature of Things that this TV host catches his own fish for chowder

David Suzuki has a slight problem. He is married to a "committed feminist," Tara Cullis. Now, there is nothing wrong with that, of course; more and more men are coping quite well with a changing world.

But please remember that David Suzuki is a Japanese Canadian. To quote the host of *The Nature of Things*: "In our family, when my father and I finished a bowl of rice, we would just hold the empty bowl up in the air and it would be immediately refilled. I remember the first Canadian girl I dated. When I did that, she said, 'What's wrong with you?' *That* is when I learned things would be different."

And indeed they are. "I have to pull my weight now!" Suzuki says today. "My wife does the cooking, but she *never* has to do a dish. *I* do all the dishwashing!"

To millions of Canadians (and millions more Americans on various cable stations), David Takayoshi Suzuki does a lot of moral, ethical, and scientific thinking as well as the dishwashing. And we are all richer for it.

Born in Vancouver on March 24, 1936, Suzuki graduated with an honours degree in biology from Amherst College, Massachusetts, and then from 1958 to 1961 went to the University of Chicago for his doctorate. He was involved in the American civil rights movement of the 1960s, worked for a year with the U. S. Atomic Energy Commission at Oak Ridge, Tennessee, after which he returned to Canada to teach at the University of Alberta in Edmonton, where he had his first brush with the mass media.

"There was a TV program, *Your University Speaks*, on Sunday mornings at 10 A.M., with an audience of about five people. They wanted any professor at the university who wouldn't freak out before the camera." You guessed it. Suzuki ended up giving about eight of the lectures, at $50 a shot, and he soon "realized that it wasn't frightening at all."

The following year, in 1963, he joined the faculty of the University of British Columbia, where he spoke about fruit flies, cloning, genetics, and such major topics. "It was my teaching," he says, "that made me aware of the tremendous abuse of genetics in the past. I started thinking that science *cannot* stay in the lab!" And who better than David Suzuki, to get science out of the lab, and into the living room/dining room/den/bedroom? He adds quickly, "I soon learned what a powerful thing TV is!"

He became a full professor of zoology at UBC in 1969 (and earned such honours as the E.W.R. Steacie Memorial Fellowship as Canada's outstanding research scientist for three consecutive years, 1969–72), and at about the same time he began hosting *Suzuki on Science* on national television. "It was on Sunday afternoons, and we had a budget of about $1,600 a week for the half-hour show. And it was up against Sunday football!" Not only that, but "it was a bunch of talking heads." Furthermore, Suzuki made it a radical program. "I was a hippie, with a headband and hair down my neck. I look back now and cringe: to wear a headband on TV!!"

But hippie or no hippie, he began to host another show, *Science Magazine*, in 1974, and that brought him to Toronto for the next decade, during which time he also hosted the popular radio series, *Quirks and Quarks*, beginning in 1975 and running for the next five years. But enough is enough: "When we made *The Nature of Things* [which grew out of *Science Magazine*] into one hour, I dropped radio."

In the meantime, life away from the camera has been busy. In 1984 his wife Tara Cullis received a professorship at Harvard, teaching Expository Writing, and she commutes between Boston and Toronto. "She is the brains of the family, with a doctorate in comparative literature from the University of Wisconsin," says no-mean-brains-himself. "We commuted two and a half

"I was a hippie, with a headband and hair down my neck"

heavy that they occasionally fall and break their legs.

David Suzuki rarely entertains, since "I'm never home." He and his wifc havc an apartment in Toronto, which they use twelve months a year, but like to spend as much time as they can in their "dream home" in the Kitsilano area of Vancouver, "right on the water."

Wife Tara is "an outstanding Chinese and Japanese cook," and Suzuki notes that "she has the hardest critics of all—my parents. And they think that she is a *terrific* Japanese cook!" (As for David Suzuki, "I know how to boil water," which isn't as minor as you think, since "my wife and I cannot get out of bed without me making a pot of tea.")

Food is always a problem, of course, for TV stars on the go. "When you film on location, you eat whenever and whatever you can. I always put on weight on a shoot." Suzuki hates North American breakfasts, with eggs and all the cholesterol, and notes that "in Newfoundland, at least you can get cod flakes, cod cheeks, cod tongues, and fishcakes." But he has kept the weight off by working out every afternoon, doing ten push-ups and 250 sit-ups, and running four to six miles a day.

Suzuki's "favourite recipe," he admits, is fish he's caught: cleaning it, shaking it up in a bag of flour, salting it, and frying it in butter until the tail and fins are crisp. "You have to sleep overnight in a tent and have the smell of fire and smoke and be hungry. The greatest condiment in the world is hunger!"

Hunger for knowledge, as well.

"When you film on location, you eat whenever and whatever you can"

years between Toronto and Wisconsin." They have two daughters under the age of five.

Over the years of hosting the widely admired *Nature of Things*, Suzuki has done a number of fascinating items on food. "The first year I did *Science Magazine*," recalls Suzuki, "I shot the introduction of one in Tanaka's of Tokyo, with me eating Japanese food. It was a program on seaweed." In the 1983–84 season he did an item on why some chicken meat is dark and some light. (It has to do with the needs of muscles: the ones that are needed for short bursts of speed are white; prolonged activity leads to darker meat.)

Years ago, Suzuki covered a "new genetic trick for breeding grains much faster. It cut breeding time in half, and it has become a very important factor around the world." And another favourite item was on doubled-muscled cows. Apparently, these giants are used as veal in Italy, and are so

Porpoise Bay Chunder

Go to the sea. Have a wonderful time catching what you can. Boil all in a pot with cut-up vegetables and dumplings, and toast your prowess as a hunter and gatherer. This is not a gourmet dish; we only make this at the cottage under primitive conditions on a Coleman stove, and it's always different. But it reheats beautifully. In fact, it improves as the flavours blend, and can be eked out deliciously for days!

Ingredients

1 live Dungeness Crab
12 cockles
3 oysters
12 mussels
12 clams, any variety
3 sea cucumbers
2 rock cod
½ lingcod
1 dozen prawns
3 carrots
2 onions
3 potatoes
Several garlic cloves
1 cup peas or anything green (i.e., green onions, etc.)
Handful of mushrooms
Dumplings (made according to your favourite recipe)
12 cherrystone clams

Instructions

At low tide, catch whatever you can of the above varieties of seafood. Prepare seafood. Clean sea cucumber—be merciless and cut off each end. Slice up the middle and open out flat. Peel 5 muscle bands from skin; keep them and discard everything else. Chop muscles into small chunks. Wash cockles, mussels, clams, and oysters. Beard the mussels (i.e., remove the byssus (fuzzy part)). Put mussels, prawns, and pieces of sea cucumber in boiling water or white wine (1 inch in the bottom of the pot). Cook 2–3 minutes with the lid on, until the shells open and the prawns begin to look opaque. Do not overcook. Discard oyster shells and all but 8 of each of the clams and mussel shells. Strain broth through several layers of cheesecloth to remove sand. Rinse clam meat, etc., for the same reason. Rinse cockles particularly carefully, removing gills if you can find them. (Hint: turn the body inside out.) Chop each cockle and oyster into 3 pieces. Put seafood and shells aside, Retain strained broth in big soup pot. Clean and fillet rock cod, scaling but not removing skin. Be careful of the spine or your hands will be sore for days. Chop fillets into 1-inch chunks. Boil crab live for 12 minutes in salted water. Discard hot water. Cool crab in cold water and break off the legs. Open the back, eat the green tamale with a spoon—YUM!—and pour the liquid and odd bits into the broth pot. Discard feathery gills and head (the tiny part behind the eyes and mouth). Break body into 4 chunks. *To prepare vegetables*: Wash and cut up all vegetables. Add several crushed garlic cloves. Add a third of the rock cod (it will disintegrate into the broth, thereby adding flavour). Add chicken broth to stretch the broth, as you'll need more broth when the balance of the seafood is added. Have your favourite dumpling recipe mixed and ready (James Beard's recipe, for example). Roll into sticky balls—your hands will be a terrible mess. Drop the balls into the soup. They should almost cover the entire surface. Turn the heat right down. Let all simmer for half-hour. Do not take the lid off until half-hour is up. While waiting, serve a dozen cherrystone clams on the half shell with cocktail sauce and cold martinis. Remove dumplings carefully—don't get tops wet. Turn up the heat and add the lingcod and the rest of the rock cod chunks. Cook for a minute or two until flesh becomes opaque. Add salt, pepper, and sugar to taste. Add seafood, including crab, and top with dumplings. Serve (as the sun sets over the sea and mountain) with thick slices of buttered bread, and plenty of cold dry white wine. If you have the facilities for a simple salad, make one, but this is not at all crucial. And *voilà*—AMBROSIA!

Wine

Anyone's dry white homemade wine of any colour except green. Failing that, chilled Muscadet de Sèvre-et-Maine.

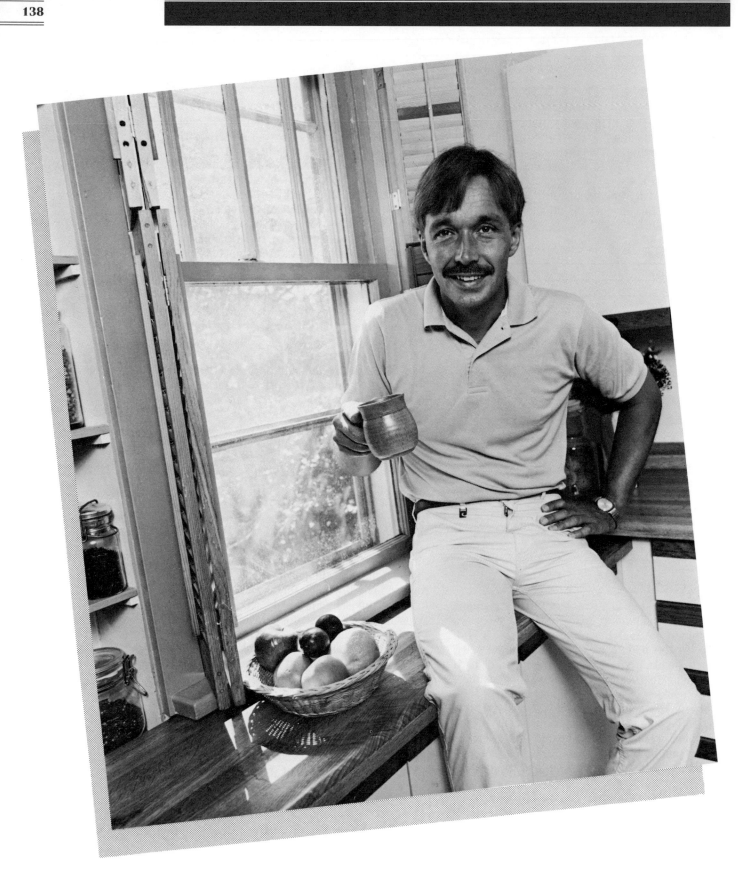

Lindy Thorsen

The host of Saskatchewan Today *knows how to serve up a Perfect Poached Egg*

*I*n this book you are reading about men and women who have risen to the top of their profession: people who are listened to, watched, admired, respected, both locally and often from coast to coast, on radio and/or TV. Some were nearly born to it; others fell in love with their medium in their teens; others fell into it by chance. Like the proverbial mountain to the mountain-climber, it was *there*.

Then there is the delightful case of Lindy Thorsen, the popular host of *Saskatchewan Today*, out of Regina. Believe it or not, he took a mail-order course in broadcasting, which taught him "to speak clearer." It was with that famous Columbia School of Broadcasting. "It cost me $600," he says. "I pull out the old audition tapes now and then, and they're a *hoot*!"

Lindy Thorsen was born on September 19, 1944, in Winnipeg. His father—who had come from Norway in 1930 and married in that prairie city—ran a gym in Vancouver for a while, but the family moved back to Winnipeg and Lindy was raised there.

He attended the University of Manitoba, starting in architecture; but when he realized that "the best I could be was a mediocre architect," he got a degree in arts, and tried teaching. From 1970 to 1973 he taught junior high English in his native city, got married in 1968, then moved out to the West Coast. But he couldn't find a job—so it was at this point that he took the correspondence course.

"With this piece of paper and three audio tapes, I managed to get a part-time and later almost-full-time position at CJVB in Vancouver." He did the 11 P.M.-to-6 A.M. shift, playing discs of a decidedly ethnic nature. "I spun the top hits from Germany, Belgium, Italy, the Ukraine—over two dozen languages. It was a multi-cultural station." Oh, he read the news in English.

After doing that for about a year, Thorsen realized that he was making only about $4 an hour. "I can't afford to do this!" he thought to himself, so he returned to teaching in 1975 and enrolled in the summer program at the University of British Columbia to obtain an M.Ed.

He took only two courses before finding another teaching job in North Vancouver. One year later he was "caught in the declining enroll-

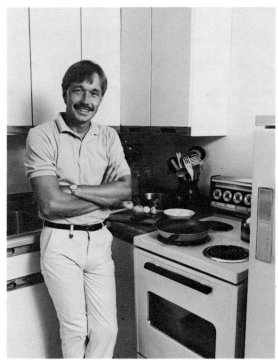

ment crunch." Six jobs were cut, including his. "I was unemployed for half a year, my marriage broke up, and I had my first life crisis."

"Everyone in Canada should go north of the 60th parallel!"

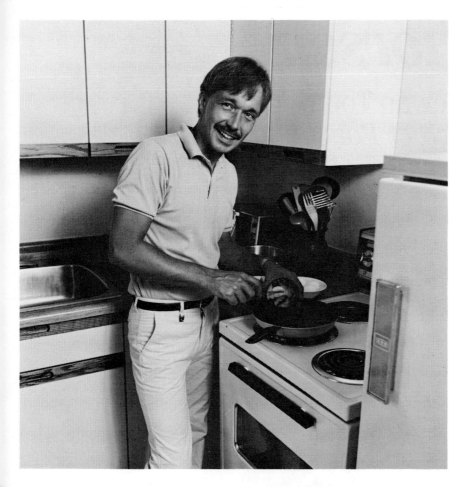

"I keep thinking I should be bored, after four years"

Thorsen spent three years in the land of rocks and stunted trees—"we were the only station to listen to"—doing the morning show, then the afternoon show. Next, a position opened in Regina to read the supper-hour TV news and he did that for three months. In July 1980 he joined the radio morning show, *Saskatchewan Today*, where he has been ever since.

"It's a *provincial* show," he underlines. "We are *not* the urban sound; we reflect the sound of the *province*." In fact, he is linked with a co-host in Saskatoon, so you get the daily mantra: "Hi! I'm Lindy Thorsen in Regina!" "Hi! I'm J. D. Lloyd in Saskatoon!"

After all those hit-and-miss years in teaching and broadcasting, Lindy Thorsen appears to have found happiness at last. "I'm happy here," he declares. "I keep thinking that I should be *bored*, after four years, but 4 A.M. is a bloody nice time to go to work!" He gets up at 3:30 A.M., starts work at 5 A.M., and is home by 1 P.M., which is probably a lot earlier than most of us get there.

Thorsen and his co-vivant prefer two or three other couples, rather than "loud parties," when they entertain. "I make *some* cookies on weekends," he says. His favourite drink is cognac; coffee is imbibed by the gallon in the morning. And he recommends The Hoist Room for "*good* steaks and baked potatoes" the next time you are in Yellowknife.

To stay in shape, Lindy Thorsen takes aerobic classes at the CBC, and he is trying hard to quit smoking. He reads books and cross-country-skis in his spare time. And even after the three years of ecstasy in the Far North, he is more than content being one of the morning voices of the prairies.

Columbia School of Broadcasting, you have a living commercial, out in Regina. He thanks you, we thank you, and the entire province of Saskatchewan thanks you. It is wonderful to know that those correspondence courses *can* work, after all.

So there Lindy Thorsen sat, collecting pogie and thinking to himself, "Well, I *did* like broadcasting . . ." He began hanging around the big CBC building in Vancouver, where he applied for the job of hauling cables and painting sets.

Then a great joy: he was hired in March 1977 to become an announcer/operator in Yellowknife, Northwest Territories. "I *loved* it!" he explodes today. "An *incredible* experience! *Everyone* in Canada should go north of the 60th parallel! The native situation is totally different!" There was a lot of travelling, and Thorsen became a technician as well as an announcer, "so it was real hands-on!"

Lindy Thorsen is a walking advertisement for the North: "Great people and great country! The lakes are beautiful! Great camping and fishing!" (Actually, he is in good literary company. One of the most delightful essays in Mordecai Richler's recent book is a wild rave about *his* loving response to Yellowknife.)

PERFECT POACHED EGG

INGREDIENTS

2 eggs
Glop of butter
Water
Salt and pepper
2 slices rye bread, toasted

INSTRUCTIONS

In a separate pot, bring to a boil enough water to fill your frying pan. Place a glop of butter in your frying pan, and set on a separate element on low, low heat—just hot enough to melt butter, not cook it. When water is boiling, lower the two eggs in for 10–12 seconds and then remove. (This helps to set the egg so it doesn't run all over when you break it into water.) Pour the water from the pot into the frying pan. Carefully crack the eggs and slip them into the water. Leave them there until the yolks cream over. Lift the eggs out with a slotted spoon so that they drain, and place each one on a slice of well-buttered rye toast. Salt and pepper to taste.
Serves 2

BEVERAGE

Cold milk in spotlessly clean, tall crystal glasses from the set your grandmother left you and you've only got three left.

OMELETTE FOR ONE

This is ideal for Saturday or Sunday morning brunches. If making for my lady, I double the recipe.

INGREDIENTS

2 strips bacon, cut in small pieces	2
$1/4$ onion, chopped	$1/4$
$1/2$ green pepper, chopped	$1/2$
6–8 mushrooms, sliced (should be fresh, not canned)	6–8
2 large eggs	2
$1/4$ cup milk	50 mL
Pinch of garlic powder	a pinch
Pinch of oregano	a pinch
1 tbsp. cold water	15 mL
$1/2$ cup cheddar cheese, grated	125 mL
Glop of butter	

INSTRUCTIONS

Combine bacon, onion, green pepper, and mushrooms in skillet, and fry till bacon is medium crisp. Remove from pan and set aside on paper towels. Clean pan. Whip together eggs, milk, garlic powder, oregano, and cold water. (The water is the secret ingredient that keeps the omelette from sticking to the pan.) Drop a large glop of butter into a medium-hot pan. Don't give it a chance to burn. Pour in egg mixture. Start shaking pan and stirring mixture immediately; keep doing so till omelette initially sets. Then start tipping uncooked egg from the centre of the pan out to the rim, and let it run around the rim till it sets well. When mixture is almost but not fully set, throw cheese in along a line through the centre of the pan. Add the bacon, onion, green pepper, and mushroom mixture on top of the cheese. Fold one side of the omelette over the ingredients. Fold second side over first, and slide omelette out of pan onto plate. I like to serve this with chilled goblet of $1/2$ cup (125 mL) orange juice, and $1/2$ cup (125 mL) Asti Spumante.
Serves 1

WINE

A half bottle of Côtes du Rhone red or Spanish Rioja—in front of the television set.

Dennis Trudeau

The host at Daybreak starts you on your way with Omelette Supreme

*L*et's get something straight, right off the top: Dennis Trudeau is *not* related to *Him*. In fact, Dennis Trudeau is not even Francophone (although, to be fair, his father's great-great-grandfather *was* French). But he *has* been in the province of Quebec for the past fifteen years, and he *can* speak French, so his name need not be *too* deceptive.

In many ways Dennis Trudeau has the classic background for the kind of a man who would fascinate, enrage, and (most especially) en*gage* radio listeners in Montreal and environs. Born in Ottawa on January 22, 1948, he attended the University of Ottawa (where he studied political science) and the University of Western Ontario in London (where he studied journalism). "I wanted to be a TV or radio host when I was in university," he says today, although it would be some years before he fulfilled that dream. He first "got the bug" when he was involved in university radio in Ottawa. But Western was the print-media school, so for the next decade, Trudeau worked in that. He spent 1970–71 in Quebec City working for the Quebec *Chronicle Telegraph*—"that's where I learned to speak French"—and then worked for Canadian Press, in that city and Montreal, from 1971 to 1974. For the next two years he covered the political and labour beats for the Montreal *Gazette*, after which he was the Quebec City correspondent for the Montreal *Star* for two years. What a great background for radio!

And it was a great time to be a reporter. The Parti Québécois had just come to power, and news had never been so newsworthy in the province. Then Trudeau had a year's fellowship to study law at Laval University, and there he learned "all about the constitution." (It was a fellowship given to various journalists.)

During all this time there was no radio or TV work in Dennis Trudeau's life—but when it came, it came quickly and heavily. In 1979 he joined CBC Radio as the host of *Quebec AM* out of Quebec City. "I walked in off the street and said, 'I heard that you might have an opening." And they said to me, 'Would you like to do it?'"

Ever modest, Trudeau notes that "I had a good voice and I knew Quebec politics." What he did *not* know was that he "had to get up at five in the morning." But that's the way the radio waves bounce. Trudeau stayed there from March of 1979 to the fall of 1980, being heard on the thirty-one English radio transmitters in the province. He also travelled the province extensively during that year-plus, and became quite well known and admired.

Then it was off to the Big City to host The Sunday morning show, *Cross Country Checkup*, about which Trudeau himself admits: "To *listen* to it, and to *do* it, is an acquired taste!" In what way, you ask? "You have to listen to people, get them to say what they have to say, and get them off the air." Easier said than done. Or, as Dennis Trudeau said, for the next two years, "You made your point. Thanks for calling!" (He also did various announcing jobs for the CBC, but this was the big one, from 1980 to 1982.)

"You have to listen to people, get them to say what they have to say and get them off the air"

Interestingly, during all that time, Trudeau never really needed to use that famous six-second delay "except once," when a caller began to use racial-religious slurs against a particular Member of Parliament. (The "six-second delay" allows a host to cut off abusive callers before their words are broadcast to the listening audience.) "People don't phone *Cross Country Checkup* to be abusive," says Dennis Trudeau. How very Canadian of them.

In 1981 the daily morning show in Montreal opened. "So I did *Daybreak* for a year, while still juggling *Cross Country Checkup*." But, as you might well imagine, "It was just too much!" Five in the morning, five days a week, followed by that Sunday stint.

Trudeau has been with the very popular *Daybreak* since 1981, the ratings are up, and he enjoys doing it. "I push people in my interviews, and don't let them say silly things," he insists. Well, *most* of the time. For instance he once interviewed Mayor Jean Drapeau, who "got away with murder! He's hypnotic; a demogogic orator! He's got you hypnotized, and then the interview is over!" Yes, even Dennis Trudeau can't handle the Expo Man.

"It's a good thing, getting up early," he rationalizes. "It keeps you out of trouble and in shape." He goes to bed "right after Knowlton and a bit of *The Journal*," and he "siestas" in the afternoon. Not that *Daybreak* is everything. There are the yearly summer stints of two weeks on *As It Happens* ("It's fun—I *love* it!").

In private life, our subject has been living with a woman for the past eleven years, and they have a four-year-old child, Samuel. He lets Suzanne do "most of the cooking." Trudeau is a seafood lover, but not a lover of hard liquor (he drinks beer and wine). He confesses to six cups of coffee on weekday mornings. And then there is that fan of the morning show who brings him a cake every year on his birthday. "A kugel one time; a birthday cake sometimes; something for Hanukkah."

"Getting up early keeps you out of trouble and in shape"

Other pleasures go by the wayside. "I gave up smoking fifty cigarettes a day, eighteen months ago—over New Year's Eve." His favourite restaurant is Nassos, on St. Lawrence Boulevard, which reportedly has "very *very* good fried squid." With kugels, birthday cakes, and fried squid, it helps that Dennis Trudeau swims three-quarters of a mile, three times a week, and diets occasionally.

Hobbies? Reading. Going to movies. "I loved *Fanny and Alexander*. And I will read *anything*." And unlike that other Trudeau, there is no retirement in sight.

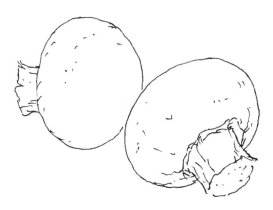

OMELETTE SUPREME

INGREDIENTS

2 eggs
Pinch of nutmeg
Bacon, precooked, crumbled
Tomato, diced
Cheese, shredded
Mushrooms, sliced

INSTRUCTIONS

Separate egg yolks from whites. Beat the whites until almost stiff; beat the yolks and add to the whites. Add nutmeg, bacon, tomatoes, cheese, and mushrooms. Pour into hot skillet. When mixture bubbles, fold in half, flip out of skillet, and serve.
Serves 1

WINE

As a lunchtime dish, a light, dry red wine like Beaujolais or Valpolicella. For dinner a more substantial red: Burgundy, Maréchal Foch. For breakfast, coffee.

ARMENIAN SALAD

INGREDIENTS

1 cup onions, finely chopped	250 mL
1 cup green peppers, finely chopped	250 mL
1 cup red peppers, finely chopped	250 mL
1 cup parsley, finely chopped	250 mL
1 14-oz can of lentils, drained	1 398-g can

INSTRUCTIONS

Mix with your favourite vinaigrette dressing. Serve chilled.
Serves 6–8

WINE

If the Liquor Board is out of Armenian red wine, a Portuguese Dão or Chilean Cabernet Sauvignon will make a good stand-in for this dish.

Wayne and Shuster

Canada's funniest duo cook up classy recipes as well as classic skits

*I*nterviewing and discussing Johnny Wayne and Frank Shuster in two separate chapters would be like doing the same with Laurel and Hardy, Abbott and Costello, or any other great comedy team. So I didn't. And encountering Wayne and Shuster in slacks instead of in costume, in-office instead of on-tube, one realizes that this is truly a marriage that was made in heaven. (Well, in Toronto.) And a marriage that has lasted about three decades more than most, and is a lot more financially and creatively successful.

They are both in their sixties now, and Johnny Wayne jumps in: "You couldn't say forty-three?" But on nearly everything else, they agree with joy and gusto.

They met in 1931 at Harbord Collegiate, one of the great Canadian high schools between the two world wars, and graduated from there together in 1936. "We were influenced by a teacher of history," says Wayne. "He wrote very funny sketches, and introduced me to *Punch* Magazine; a wonderful, funny man." Not surprisingly, the two men instituted an award in his name at their old high school alma mater.

W. and S. were in the same classes through high school, playing in Gilbert and Sullivan (another great team) operettas and they continued their obsession with and passion for the British musical team into their television years.

At the University of Toronto they were both in English together—"pretty much in the same classes," notes Shuster, and went on to the School of Graduate Studies for a nearly reached M.A., until "we got a job in the war." "Frank has the M., I have the A.," says Johnny Wayne. And note their routine when they mention World War II: "You've heard about the war?" asks Shuster. "It was in all the papers," concludes Wayne. (They did the famed U.C. Follies at U. of T., by the way—"the classiest show of its time," adding that "Leacock was doing it before us," and then they were shipped off to be infantry officers in the Canadian Army.)

But not for long. An impresario wanted to create an army show, so W. and S. wrote the music, book, and lyrics—"*most* of the songs"—and they played across Canada for civilians and the military. "It was to give the Canadian Army the image of being bright, intellectually fun, and entertaining," says one of them, I forget which just now. "The New York *Times* said that *The Canadian Army Show* was better than their country's *This is the Army*," announces Wayne proudly.

When the cast of 300 (!) was taken to Europe to play to the troops, it was broken into five self-sustaining and portable units. "Frank and I wrote the five unit productions," recalls Wayne, "and we toured the European bases. My unit was selected to go to Normandy on D plus forty [days]."

"The New York Times *said that* The Canadian Army Show *was better than their country's* This Is The Army*"*

They would set up in a field with their own generator. They played towns where the power had been wiped out; in one place they performed in a cave that had been used by the Nazis as an ammunition dump. They even played in the casino in Deauville where Sara Bernhardt and Maurice Chevalier had once performed (in quieter times).

By early 1945, as the war ran down, so did Wayne and Shuster's great army career. But then they were approached by the Department of Veteran Affairs to do a radio show that would "explain all the benefits being introduced by the government" to the men returning home. The radio program was called *The Johnny Home Show*. (Remember that, Dad?) It ran from 1945 to 1946 on radio, "won many prizes," and it was written by (but did not star) Johnny Wayne and Frank Shuster. Some of you may remember the voices of such stars as Austin Willis and Bernie Braden.

In 1947 came the *Wayne and Shuster Show* on CBC radio, which followed the *Kraft Music Show* and which rapidly became the top-rated radio show in this country. In 1948 they did a summer replacement for NBC's *The Life of Reilly* for thirteen weeks, which they (typically) asked to do out of Toronto. "We were the first people in this country with our names on a show," Johnny recalls. And it's true: think of all the brand names of those old radio shows, and then think of the *W. and S. Show*.

And how can you *stop* thinking of the Wayne and Shuster shows, or team? For these men have not been off the airwaves of Canada and the United States (and, more recently, the earth) since 1954—three full decades! (And there were some pretty busy years there: in 1954 alone, for instance, they did thirty-nine radio shows and six half-hour TV shows.)

And of course there was Ed Sullivan. From 1958 to 1971 the Canadian comics appeared on his show sixty-seven times—a record that no one even comes close to, with some sketches running up to eighteen minutes on a program where five minutes was the norm, and even the rule.

Both members of the team have found time for a full private life. Johnny Wayne is the proud father of Brian Wayne (a producer/director of CBC Sports), Jamie Wayne (an author, journalist, and contributing editor of *The Financial Post*), and Michael Wayne, a distinguished historian of American history (which is only somewhat ironic, from the oldest son of a man who flatly refused to leave Canada, the way so many other world-class stars have done). Wayne's wife Bea passed away recently, but his oldest son has presented him with a new granddaughter, Beatrice, to commemorate her name and memory.

Frank Shuster is the proud father of Rosalynd (Rosie) Shuster, who used to be one of the key writers for *Saturday Night Live* during its halcyon days and nights, and who now commutes between New York and Los Angeles, working on screen plays. He also has a son, Steve Shuster, a musician/comedian who often performs at Yuk Yuks in Toronto and other nightclubs. Frank's wife Ruth is an interior designer.

When I asked W. and S. to recall their favourite food sketches, one that quickly came to mind was *The Picture of Dorian Wayne*, from back in the early 1960s. In it, a man sold his soul so that he could eat as much as he wanted. "The picture got fat," recalls Shuster gleefully. Sir Hubert Fresser was played by Shuster, naturally. "The picture frame breaks at the end of the sketch," says Wayne, but in the last scene, you may recall, Johnny Wayne descends the stairs, as slim as could be. We should all be so lucky.

Once, in fact, Wayne and Shuster did a whole show dedicated to the Wonderful World of Food. For instance, do you recall how pizza was invented? Florence was being attacked by Milan, and the defenders of the city ran out of stones. And all they had around was flour, cheese, pepperoni....(You guessed: it was all dropped off the wall and the enemy was slaughtered.)

Or that other great moment when that huge salad was being created for Julius Caesar, in which the chef threw in romaine lettuce, anchovies, eggs, croutons, Romano cheese...."'What shall we call this salad, Caesar?' 'I'll call it—Cole Slaw'!"

But the tastes of these two giants of comedy run to more than cole slaw. Johnny Wayne, for instance, used to spend every May visiting three-star restaurants in France and Italy. "I taught myself Italian, so I can read any menu. I speak 'culinary Italian.'" He adds that he loves Italian food and makes "a *wonderful* pesto out of basil that I grow myself."

To which the more gourmand Shuster adds, "I love Italian food, too. I also love triple-cut lamb chops. Oh, I'll eat *everything*!"

Wayne is a connoisseur of wines as well,

"especially the *beautiful* Italian wines of Piemonte and Toscana, and the wines of Alsace and Burgundy too!" Shuster is a martini man, and a true fan of the Zombie. "I sip it carefully. That *is* a good drink!"

In Toronto, Johnny Wayne recommends Sabatino's, a fine Italian restaurant near his home, and Shuster gives a plug to The Four Seasons in New York. And the ultimate? Johnny Wayne, the food maven, recommends Alain Chapel, outside Lyon, France, in Mionnay—"unbelievable!"

As for diet, Shuster, speaking for both, notes that "we've never *stopped* being careful. We watch our diets *all* our lives. TV puts on pounds, and the costume people are always telling you, 'You're putting it on!'"

But, adds his partner, "The nature of this business keeps you active. You have to keep in shape. We do physical things in our comedy, including falls."

Physical things, perhaps, but never a complete fall, at least in our hearts and the TV ratings. And ditto for tens of millions on five continents and in over two dozen countries around the world who regularly tune into Wayne and Shuster—the two childhood chums who have remained true to their home and native land, and true to the ideals of good humour and comedy, for over thirty years.

"We were the first people in this country with our names on a show"

RICE CASSEROLE

(*Frank Shuster*)

INGREDIENTS

2 cups long grain rice (mix brown with wild rice, if desired)	500 mL
1 cup Spanish onion, diced	250 mL
1 cup butter	250 mL
2 cups fresh mushrooms, sliced	500 mL
Salt and pepper to taste	
Pinch of oregano (optional)	a pinch
1 10-oz. can water chestnuts, thinly sliced	1 284-mL can

INSTRUCTIONS

Preheat oven to 350°F (180°C). Prepare rice as per package instructions. Cook until slightly firm. Sauté onions in half the butter. When golden, add mushrooms and sauté until slightly cooked. Add mushrooms and onions to rice. Mix well. Add remaining butter, salt, and pepper to taste, oregano (if desired), and mix. Add water chestnuts and mix thoroughly. Place mixture in buttered casserole, cover, and bake for approximately 1 to 1½ hours, until edges begin to brown. (If too dry, add a small amount of water.)

WINE

A good red wine is required to help you forget that there is no meat in this dish: Italian Barbaresco or Merlot.

PESTO PRESTO

(Johnny Wayne)

INGREDIENTS

2 cups fresh basil leaves	500 mL
2 tbsp. pine nuts	30 mL
1 clove garlic, crushed	1
1/2 cup olive oil	125 mL
1 tsp. salt	5 mL
1/2 cup Parmesan cheese, grated	125 mL
2 tbsp. Romano cheese, grated	30 mL
3 tbsp. softened butter	45 mL

INSTRUCTIONS

In a food processor or blender, blend basil leaves, pine nuts, garlic, olive oil, and salt at high speed. Stop from time to time to push mixture down with spatula. Add cheeses and blend. Add butter and blend. Then take the delightful green mixture and spoon it over hot pasta.
Serves 6

WINE

A Northern Italian red from Tuscany or Piedmont. Make sure your partner eats the pesto, too. Otherwise, accompany with mouthwash.

CARAMEL APPLE-PEAR PIE

(Frank Shuster)

INGREDIENTS

2 1/8 cups all-purpose flour	530 mL
1/2 tsp. salt	2 mL
1/2 cup butter	125 mL
1/2 cup shortening	125 mL
4 1/2 tbsp. cold water	65 mL
4 medium Spy apples	4
Juice 1 small lemon	1
1/4 cup flour	50 mL
1/2 cup light brown sugar (depending on tartness of apples)	125 mL
2 tbsp. butter	30 mL
2 14-oz. cans pears, drained	2 398-mL cans
1/2 cup Kraft Caramels, cut-up	125 mL

INSTRUCTIONS

To prepare pastry: Sift flour 3 times, add salt, and cut in butter and shortening until pieces are the size of peas. Add water and mix until dough holds together. Handling dough as little as possible, form into a ball, divide in half, and keep in refrigerator until ready to use.
To prepare filling: Peel and slice apples. Place in bowl and add lemon juice. Preheat oven to 425°F (220°C). Roll dough out on lightly floured board. Line buttered 10-inch (25-cm) pie plate with dough. Sprinkle with half the flour. Arrange one layer of apples on top. Sprinkle with half the brown sugar, and dot with butter. Add a layer of sliced pears and caramel pieces on top. Repeat the flour, apples (including lemon juice), sugar, butter, pears, and caramel pieces pattern—piling the fruit highest in the centre. Cover with pastry, pinching the top and bottom dough together. Cut several slits in the top pastry. Bake about one hour, reducing oven temperature to 350°F (180°C) after the first 15 minutes of baking, until centre is tender and crust golden brown. Serve warm with either ice cream or Cheddar cheese—or both.
Serves 8

BEVERAGE

The eau-de-vie Pear William, the dry, distilled essence of the fruit—Rieder makes it in Ontario —unless you plan a pie fight, in which case have soap and water on hand.

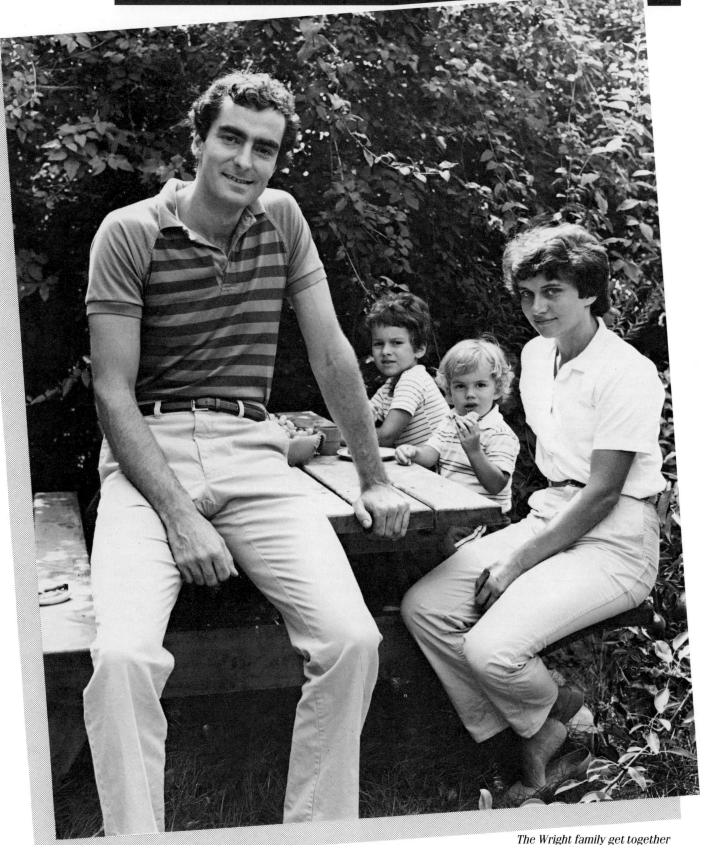

The Wright family get together for a picnic. (Left to right) Jim, Ian, Nicholas, and Anne.

Jim Wright

Appropriately, the host of The Entertainers was once a Circus Ringmaster

*I*f you have ever assumed that working for the Canadian Broadcasting Corporation must be like living in a circus, you must therefore assume that Jim Wright, the host of CBC Radio's popular *The Entertainers*, was just *made* for the job. For, as he likes to point out, "I'm the only person I know who has "Circus Ringmaster' on my résumé."

What happened was that Wright spotted a notice on a theatre bulletin board advertising for a circus ringmaster. The pay was $400 a week, the tour would last seven months—in the world of theatre, that's known as a rather long run—and the company was Canada's only circus, Garden Brothers. He took along his new wife and travelled 20,000 miles over the next half-year.

Memories? How about the chaotic 22,000 screaming kids in the Montreal Forum, where he had to do the show in both official languages? "You are the stage manager as well as announcer," he recalls. But was he nervous? Let's put it this way: he lost fifteen pounds during the first two weeks of the job. (The Quick Weight Loss Terror Diet.)

All this would be slightly less eccentric, were it not for the fact that Jim Wright comes from the most traditional of backgrounds. Born in Newmarket, Ontario, just north of Toronto, on June 28, 1949, he went to St. Andrew's College, where his father taught and also served as head of the Junior School. Then Wright, Sr., founded a boy's day school in Toronto, along the lines of Upper Canada College, called St. George's College. Son Jim went off to Lakefield College School, near Peterborough.

All pretty straight, you'll have to agree. Until Wright went off to York University, from 1968 to 1972, and got neck deep into theatre. He ran a student theatre group—"The Company"—based on the radical theories of Polish director Grotowski. "It was the '60s, and things were wild!" remembers Jim Wright. He was co-director; the

other director, Jim Purdy, went on to be the creator and writer of CBC-TV's hit series, *Home Fires*.

His theatre interest was not merely a student fling. After he returned from his "compulsory European tour," he worked in the Studio Lab Theatre of Toronto, one of the more interesting and daring alternate theatres in the early 1970s. "I worked in every capacity—director, actor, producer, manager." And, during this time and earlier, Wright worked for the CBC as a summer relief announcer, and did a brief stint in Montreal, doing ten minutes of news to Africa (!) at 3 A.M.

He even started his own theatre company in Peterborough, Ontario, back in 1975: Otonabee Theatre, creating a show based on Susannah Moodie's famous study of her pioneer life in the province, *Roughing It in the Bush*. It toured local schools before Jim Wright found himself touring Canada with that crazy circus deal.

"I worked in every capacity—director, actor, producer, manager"

And speaking of crazy, the CBC invited Wright to return to the fold as a full-time temporary. And they got him at a good time, too: "The experience in the circus gave me *tremendous* experience as an announcer, and a lot of confidence, which I had lacked previously."

So Wright did *As It Happens*, replacing Allan Maitland for three months; following that, he did *Radio Noon* in Toronto for another eight months —during a provincial election. After that came *Night Nationals*, at 10 P.M. each evening. The biggest break of all was a call to do *Morningside* in the summer of 1978, replacing Don Harron during the annual hiatus. "It was a *real* opportunity for me!"

"What I really enjoy is gardening. I am a wicked compost piler!"

Home is where the heart is, however. He's devoted to his wife Anne, five-year-old Ian, and two-year-old Nicholas. Cooking, however, is not a hobby: "What I really enjoy is gardening. I am a *wicked* compost piler!"

But there *are* food anecdotes, thanks to his stint on *The Food Show*, back in the late '70s. Jim Wright recalls with great affection "the story about the man who would collect dead animals off the road and eat them. It was meat freshly killed, no chemical additives or antibiotics added. He knew exactly how it got killed, and what he was getting. Muskrat, possum, dog—it was grotesque!"

He was right. It led straight to *The Entertainers* and *The Food Show*, both of which he juggled, from 1978 to 1980. When *Arts National* came along, he did two years of *that*. And then the drive-home show of Toronto, *4 to 6*.

And finally, in the fall of 1983, Jim Wright was asked by executive producer Barbara Judges to rejoin *The Entertainers*, for which he negotiated a role as not only the host but a producer in the Variety Department as a whole. "It's the kind of role I've been looking for, for a long time," he admits.

As one can imagine, the spread of interviews is broad, and fascinating. A favourite one was with evangelist Billy Graham ("That was a big thrill; I challenged him in new areas"); a disappointing one was with the great singer Ella Fitzgerald ("I asked the same old questions, and it was a disastrous interview"). More recently, a trip to England lassoed Glenda Jackson, Stewart Granger, and the late James Mason.

Another grotesque moment on the same show was when Wright and his producers and writers played an April Fool's joke on their listeners. They "interviewed" a woman who raised budgies, slaughtered them, stuffed them, and sold them as "Bite-Sized Budgies." "Kind of a frozen TV dinner," chuckles Wright. "Did I get letters! I had *said* it was an April Fool's gag! Some burned in my hand! One man was furious that he had been taken in by us!" But that experience in the circus has prepared Jim Wright for *anything*.

ORGANIC COMPOST

The best recipe starts with fresh, untainted produce—and the best way to grow that organic produce is with organic compost. It's the best growing medium, and the fastest way to get compost is the 14-day "Hot Pile" way. Start with a 3-by-3-by-3-foot enclosure of chicken wire (for pile to air, preferably 3 feet off the ground, too). Collect bags of grass and leaves from the neighbourhood. When sufficient amounts have been collected, build a pile, alternating layers about 3 inches thick—i.e., 1 bag grass, 1 bag leaves, etc. A thin layer of soil in between gets things moving, but isn't absolutely necessary. Pile should heat up within 3 days, and will be hot to the touch inside. Pile should be kept moist, but not wet. Turn the heap every 3 days to generate air for the composting action to continue. If everything has gone well, you'll have finished the compost in 14 days.

BLACK CURRANT JAM

This is a dynamite black currant jam that my wife makes from our bushes in the garden.

INGREDIENTS

Black currants	
Water	
Sugar	
Parafin wax	

INSTRUCTIONS

Pick currants when very black and slightly soft. Boil fruit for 10 minutes in an equal amount of water. Add an equal amount of sugar to the cooked fruit. Cook for 10 minutes more. Pour into sterilized jars and cover with parafin wax.

BEVERAGE

Tea and crumpets and good conversation. If bored, lonely, or depressed, tune into *The Entertainers*.

CHRISTMAS CAKE

INGREDIENTS

1 cup butter	250 mL
1 cup granulated sugar	250 mL
3 eggs	3
3 cups all-purpose flour	750 mL
1 tsp. baking powder	5 mL
2 tsp. vanilla extract	10 mL
2 tsp. almond extract	10 mL
2 tsp. lemon extract	10 mL
1 lb. golden raisins	500 g
1 lb. candied cherries	500 g
1/4 lb. candied orange peel	125 g
1/2 lb. coconut, shredded	250 g
1 cup crushed pineapple	250 mL
1/2 cup warm water	125 mL

INSTRUCTIONS

Cream butter and sugar until light and fluffy. Beat in eggs, one at a time, until light. Combine flour and baking powder and add alternately with pineapple and water combined. Stir in flavourings. Fold in fruits and coconut. Spread in a greased and floured 9-by-13-inch (3.5 L) pan and bake for 2 hours at 275°F (140°C) with a can of water in the oven.

WINE

The perfect mate is sweet Champagne (it will probably say Doux or Demi-Doux on the label), or Asti Spumante.

Elite Confections BLUEBERRY CHARLOTTE

A blueberry charlotte is a versatile dessert, appropriate as the crowning touch for a formal dinner or for more casual entertaining. It is a light bavarois made with a purée and fresh fruit, encased in a palisade of ladyfingers.

LADYFINGERS INGREDIENTS

6 egg whites	6
3 egg yolks	3
1¼ cups icing sugar	300 mL
¼ tsp. salt	1 mL
¾ cup all-purpose flour, sifted	175 mL
½ tsp. vanilla extract	2 mL

INSTRUCTIONS

Separate eggs and save 3 yolks for the recipe below. Whip egg whites and salt to a soft-peak stage. Gradually add 1 cup (250 mL) sugar and continue beating until stiff but not dry. Combine yolks, ¼ cup (50 mL) sugar, and vanilla and beat until thick. Fold half of the yolk mixture and half of the flour into whites. Then fold in the rest. Pipe mixture onto parchment-covered cookie sheets, forming 4-inch-long (10-cm) fingers and bake at 350°F (180°C) for 15–20 minutes. Ladyfingers should be golden brown in colour.

BLUEBERRY BAVAROIS INGREDIENTS

3 egg yolks	3
⅓ cup sugar	75 mL
1 cup milk	250 mL
1 tsp. vanilla extract	5 mL
1½ tbsp. unflavoured gelatin	25 mL
2 cups whipping cream	500 mL
⅓ cup icing sugar	75 mL
1 pt. blueberries*	500 mL
1 tsp. lemon juice	5 mL
¾ cup apricot jam	175 mL

*Substitute other fresh fresh fruit in season, such as peaches, raspberries, or strawberries.

INSTRUCTIONS

Beat yolks and sugar until thick. Bring the milk and vanilla to a boil, then add slowly to yolk mixture, beating constantly. Place combined mixture back on the stove and cook at medium heat until mixture coats the back of a spoon. Remove from stove. Soften gelatin in a little water, then pour into the milk mixture and stir to dissolve. Set in a bowl of ice water, stirring occasionally. Wash the blueberries and set 12 aside for decoration. Purée ¾ cup (175 mL) of blueberries with lemon juice and add to the cold mixture. Reserve remaining blueberries for the centre of the charlotte. Whip the cream and icing sugar until stiff. Fold thickened sauce into the whipping cream until completely incorporated. *To assemble*: Place ladyfingers in bottom and sides of a 9-in. (23-cm) cake pan. Fill with layers of bavarois and blueberries, ending with the bavarois. Cover with ladyfingers and refrigerate for at least 2 hours. Turn charlotte out onto cake plate. Bring apricot jam to a boil and brush onto sides and top of charlotte. Decorate with whipping cream and blueberries. Refrigerate until ready to serve.

WINE

In keeping with the lightness and elegance of this mouth-watering dessert, a sweet Champagne or Asti Spumante.

Recipe courtesy of Richard Pattison, Elite Confections, Toronto.

Index

Photographers

David Walton: pp. 22–24, 26–28, 30–32, 38–40, 66–68, 78–80, 82–84, 90–92, 106, 108, 114, 116, 118–20, 122, 126, 130–32, 134, 135 (bottom), 147–50, 152–54.

Others: pp. 10–12: Frank Grant; p. 14: Fran Drabit; p. 16: T.G. Johns; p. 18: Fred Phipps (CBC); p. 20: Steven Bonisteel; p. 34: Fred Phipps (CBC); p. 36: courtesy of *Farm and Country*; pp. 42 and 44: Liam Sharp; pp. 46 and 48: Murray MacGowan; p. 50: CBC; p. 52: Richard Swiecki; pp. 54 and 56: Fred Phipps (CBC); p. 58: Larry Goldstein; p. 59: Bev Olandt; p. 60: Hugh Patterson; p. 62: CBC; p. 63: George Eimarrson; p. 64: Gerry Kopelow Photographics, Inc.; p. 70: Tim Harvey; pp. 71 and 72: Richard Swiecki; p. 74: CBC; p. 76: David Street; pp. 86 and 88: Craig Mackie; pp. 94–96*: Paul J. Hoeffler; pp. 98 and 100: John Lewis; p. 102: Rolfe Vracar; p. 104: CBC; pp. 110 and 112: Gerry Boland, Studio II; pp. 123, 124 (bottom), 125, and 127: Michael Cooper; p. 124 (top): Dimitri Mavrikis; p. 136: Fred Phipps (CBC); pp. 138–40: Richard Gustin; pp. 142 and 144: Michel Rouette; p. 146: Fred Phipps (CBC).

*Photographed in Linda Barr's kitchen with artifacts courtesy of John Black

About the Authors

Stephen Epstein

Bernard Gluckstein

Allan Gould, the author (and recipe-gatherer) of *Air Fare*, has long been known to CBC television and radio fans. Since the mid-1970s he has broadcast regularly on *Morningside* and *Anybody Home?*, (he was "True Facts Gould"), and has written and performed spots on *The Entertainers* and *Sunday Morning*. On CBC-TV (where he had to dress up a bit more) he was a weekly regular on *Take 30* for five years, discussing great moments and personalities in history.

Gould is also a frequent contributer to many Canadian magazines, including *Chatelaine, Canadian Business, Financial Post, TV Guide, Toronto Life, En Route, Canadian Living, Homemaker's, Quest*, and, of course, the CBC *Radio Guide*. He is the author of *The Toronto Book*, a tourist guide to his city, and *Letters I've Been Meaning to Write*, a book of humour and satire.

Married and the father of two children, Gould can't wait to try out these various recipes.

How about you?

Tony Aspler is the author of *Vintage Canada* and the wine columnist for the Toronto *Star*. He has written several novels and is a regular broadcaster on the CBC. He has been writing about wine for ten years and has contributed to *Saturday Night, Toronto Life, Beverage Canada, Wine Tidings*, and *Canadian Business*.